PRIMITIVE LABOUR

PRIMITIVE LABOUR

BY

L. H. DUDLEY BUXTON, M.A.

KENNIKAT PRESS
Port Washington, N. Y./London

PRIMITIVE LABOUR

First published in 1924
Reissued in 1971 by Kennikat Press
Library of Congress Catalog Card No: 70-115315
ISBN 0-8046-1106-8

Manufactured by Taylor Publishing Company   Dallas, Texas

PREFACE

My especial thanks are due to my friend and former tutor, Dr. R. R. Marett, for suggestions while I was writing this little book, for help with the manuscript, and for the great care with which he read the proofs. Much that appears in these pages was collected while I was travelling round the world holding the Fellowship munificently endowed by M. Albert Kahn of Paris, and I can never sufficiently express my thanks for the opportunities provided by this fellowship.

MORLEY, ALBERTA
September, 1924

CONTENTS

PART I

SPECIALIZATION OF LABOUR

PART II

NATURAL CONDITIONS OF LABOUR

PART III

TYPES AND STAGES OF LABOUR

PART I
SPECIALIZATION OF LABOUR

CHAPTER I

INTRODUCTION

The Scope of the Inquiry and the Methods of Study

THE picture of a man cast on a desert island, with no resources but the natural products of the soil and his own two hands, has been a favourite subject for the speculations of writers of fiction, most of whom have cut the Gordian knot by supplying the convenient wreck of a ship or other material advantage to the poor castaway. It is possible, however, to study the method whereby man has developed his culture, not perhaps from that shadowy time when he ceased to be an ape and became a man, but at least from a time when his material resources were very limited. We can study the origin of invention from two points of view as archæologists or as ethnologists; in the former case we must rely on the evidence of the fragments that remain from a remote period in man's history; in the latter we can visit and observe the culture of tribes who have proved but backward scholars in the arts of life.

Within recent years, perhaps more than ever before, civilized man has had occasion to dig deeply into the surface of the earth, to secure adequate foundations for big buildings, to make the roads and streets of

3

cities, and to quarry clay and sand for building. Agriculture also, especially in those countries where civilization is most deeply rooted, has turned over the earth's surface to a considerable extent with the ploughshare. During these manifold labours man has occasionally exposed the remains of his predecessors, sometimes extremely ancient, sometimes comparatively modern. Often the archæologist has gained great treasures, more frequently only fragmentary remains have rewarded his researches. Sufficient material has, however, now been collected to enable the student to reconstruct, in a comparatively complete way, the remains of bygone stages of culture.

At the same time travellers have been industriously traversing the habitable globe so that there remain few tribes, however isolated, whose culture has not been examined, at least summarily. We have, therefore, at our disposal not only the actual weapons that our early ancestors used, but also their survivals among primitive tribes. These interesting and valuable documents are no longer placed on a dusty shelf of a museum labelled, if labelled at all, " Curiosities from the South Sea Islands," but are carefully studied and, most valuable of all, are accompanied by careful accounts of their use, made by observers in the field, and by photographs which throw the greatest light on the methods of the primitive craftsman.

The archæologist and the ethnologist can, not infrequently, work together and summon, if necessary, the expert opinion of the geographer. We can sometimes recognize among primitive peoples a tool or weapon, which perhaps in an identical or slightly modified form was in use in Europe before the dawn of history. In many cases observations made on modern tools enable us to reconstruct parts of ancient tools which were made of a perishable material which has long since disappeared. In this way, for instance, by comparing the method of hafting stone axes among modern primitive races we can see how the neolithic celt was in all probability hafted by its maker. The analogy, of course, must not be pressed too closely; there may often be different conditions or converging lines of evolution which are misleading if we draw a parallel over hastily, but the general statement holds good.

In early times when the general level of culture was low, most arts were fairly wide-spread and seem to have had a fairly continuous distribution. To-day there are widely different cultures, scattered over the globe with a continuous or, in the case of the less developed, a discontinuous distribution. The same inventive genius which has enabled man to triumph over his surroundings has made him singularly anxious to adopt other people's inventions when they seem good to him. Culture-contact is therefore masking inventions and making it often difficult to disentangle the original elements of certain cultures. The lower may borrow from the higher; matches, for instance, seem to precede the explorer into the untrodden depths of the wilderness; or the higher may borrow from the lower and the heir of all the ages, the culture of the west, adopts Indian corn, cocoa, quinine and tobacco from the Indians they profess to despise.

It is extremely difficult to find people living in a state of culture which has not been affected by the missionary, the trader, the explorer or the official, and these activities are by no means limited to the white man—so that a culture is always changing not only by its own initiative, but also owing to forces acting from the outside. Our impressions, therefore, of peoples may be very erroneous if they are based on specimens in museums, which have been collected at various times, or from accounts of observers which were written at different dates.

Side by side with this adaptive tendency is an innate conservatism which is opposed to all form of change and which rejects the inventions of others and prefers to adhere to the old out-of-date inventions of past generations. Yet another factor must be taken into consideration, the imitative faculty of man, a faculty which also seems to be highly developed in his nearest relations in the animal kingdom. Owing to this faculty he will sometimes take over an invention and copy its externals slavishly, without in any way understanding their true import. A most remarkable instance of this is reported by Williams in Papua,[1] where the natives constructed most ingeniously out of cane a complete model of a wireless aerial and masts, with a cabin for an operator at each end, apparently with the idea of getting wireless messages from their ancestors who were supposed to be returning to earth !

When we are dealing with living peoples these culture-contacts in relation to inventions are sometimes not difficult to work out; in dealing with extinct peoples they are very complicated and have often led to wide controversies, taking the extreme form of theories which uphold, on the one hand, the independent invention of various devices in widely scattered parts of the world, and, on the other, the wide distribution of certain elements of a single culture affecting much of the world. As an example of the latter the recent theories of Professor Elliot Smith in regard to

[1] F. E. Williams' Report on the Anthropology of Papua, " The Vallala Madness."

heliolithic culture, which will be discussed later, may
be taken as the most striking which have recently been
put forward. In regard to the former the fire-piston
used to-day in Malaysia forms a curious example.

The widely differentiated nature of modern cultures
compared with those of more primitive times raises
an important question which has its political as well
as its purely scientific aspect, namely, the relationship
of race to invention. Some have asserted that certain
races are comparatively incapable of the intellectual
effort required to perfect a new invention however
simple; others with equal force declare that the
differentiation of culture is the result of environment
rather than of race. The cranial capacity of some of
the early races of Europe has been asserted to be
greater than that of the average European to-day, a
statement that must be received with caution as the
figures on which this estimate is based are far too few
for so wide a generalization. Moreover it has by no
means been proved that there is a close correlation
between the size of the brain case and intellectual
ability.[1]

The argument about the intellectual capacity of
primitive man can be of little value, as it is obviously
impossible to estimate the comparative value of a
series of inventions which have followed one another
in an evolutionary scale, since it was the invention of
the first boat which ultimately made our modern
battleships possible. The question of the comparative
intelligence of modern primitive races is, however, of
considerable value because, could we answer it, we
should be in a position to state why certain races have

[1] The relation of cranial capacity in relation to intellect is
discussed by Professor Sollas in "Ancient Hunters," p. 158.
See also Reid and Mulligan, Journ. Roy. Anthrop. Inst., 1923.

lagged so far behind in the struggle for material advantages. The touchstone is difficult. Most of us would no doubt consider that western civilization and western inventions represent the highest point in the evolutionary scale which has so far been reached by man. The majority of Chinese scholars do not, I believe, hold that view, but consider that Chinese civilization, which on the whole is less material, is of a far higher order. It is clear if we consider the evolution of the arts of life, the western world has progressed far further than any other race.

Professor Wood Jones in his interesting book on the human hand has drawn attention to the fact that the hand, in itself, represents a comparatively primitive type of mammalian and indeed of vertebrate hand, and that the specialized extremities of the horse and the cow are much more highly developed in the evolutionary sense than our own hands. But with our simple hand we can perform the most elaborate actions. We have developed an opposable thumb, but otherwise our hand is a simple tool. It is governed by a very elaborate controlling mechanism, the brain and central nervous system. It seems not improbable that this system has differentiated among different races, but at present its anthropology is but little understood.

It has been asserted that the round-headed people of Europe are more industrious and that the long heads are more inventive. If this were true our study would be immensely simplified, as we should have to limit our search to long-headed people, among whom we should find the origin of all invention. Unfortunately the matter is far from being proved, and it still remains necessary to search the globe to discover the earliest inventors or, in default of them, the present users of those simple instruments on which all our arts are founded. Much will depend on other aspects than the psychological, the material to hand, the climate and innumerable other factors which can be observed; and therefore, for the present at least, it would seem better to abandon the shadowy path which attempts to disentangle the intellectual capacities of various races for invention and to follow other and, for the moment, surer trails.

Even these trails will, however, lead us far afield unless we define very closely what type of crafts we are going to study, and how far we are going to pursue them in their evolutionary progress. Speaking in general terms there may be said to be three stages in the development of man's culture—savagery, barbarism and finally civilization. Though it is not difficult to find typical examples of these three stages, they shade into one another and numerous exceptions can be found to any general definition.

We may define the first of the three categories very generally as being a stage of culture which is dependent on oral tradition to hand on the knowledge gained by one generation to the next. The charts of Polynesians, the drawings of various peoples may be quoted against this definition, but on the whole it will convey the general position of craftsmanship and the level of culture in such communities. It will not serve to distinguish primitive man from barbaric man where he also is dependent on oral tradition; we must therefore add the further qualification that the savage not only has no satisfactory method except by speech of publishing his ideas, but also has no means of acquiring more wealth than he can carry about on his person or on the persons of his family. The barbaric man is the man who possesses material wealth but no form of writing. Civilized man, who can write, hands on from generation to generation not only the torch of life but also material wealth and the written record of his thoughts and achievements.[1]

We are dealing with the first two stages, that of savagery and barbarism. In limiting ourselves to the arts of life, we are restricting ourselves to the inventions which are directly aimed at securing the livelihood of the savage. These arts may be defined briefly as follows : A primitive family must first of all procure something to eat and must dress it when found. This collection of raw foodstuffs and their preparation forms the most important of the arts of life. Secondly, defence against wild animals and enemies must be secured. Thirdly, man must find somewhere to live, and he must also find a means of protection against the weather when he walks abroad.

In the preparation of food and in the wearing of clothing man differs from the other animals and, for the most part, his defences are also different. He does not depend on the strength of tooth or claw; the apes are reported to use stones or sticks for defence, and even civilized man has been known to descend to these primitive weapons, but for the most part man fashions himself tools either of these two primitive materials or, as his power of invention develops, of raw materials which are more difficult to work. He has therefore been described by Tylor as being a " tool-making " rather than a tool-using animal.

There are other activities which the savage considers equally necessary to life, although they are not within our present purview. Relaxation and play forms a part of man's life at all stages of development,

[1] E. B. Tylor, " Anthropology," p. 23.

and many of the finest arts of human life are concerned with the furtherance of pleasure and relaxation.

Finally, the spiritual side of life is always with primitive man. He does not consider it enough merely to fashion and to possess implements of hunting or household gear; it does not suffice merely to plant corn or to build houses. Some means must be taken to ensure the success of the huntsman and the fertility of the crops by approaching the non-material world. "Unless the Lord build the house, their labour is but lost that build it."

There are other arts of life which are concerned with the factors which we have mentioned above, but which deserve a separate treatment. By far the most important are those concerned with transport both by water and by land, and the arts connected with trade so that the supply of the necessary commodities may be ensured and the unused surplus of others may not be wasted.

All these primitive crafts may be studied in various ways. We may take a single industry and examine its history and evolution from the most primitive form to the most elaborate. A good example may be found in the evolution of one type of potting. It is possible by smearing a basket with clay to make it water-tight, and if, either accidentally or of design, the basket is put on the fire the wicker burns away and the clay remains hard and water-tight.

Some peoples, the Indians in Mexico, for instance, to-day build up pots by coiling round strips of clay in a spiral till a complete vessel is obtained, a method which suggests very forcibly the coiling of the withes in some of their basketry. The same Indians have a primitive type of wheel which is sometimes used, although they are by no means so dependent on this wheel as the modern potter. The lump of clay on which the clay is being built up in a spiral is placed on the bottom of an old broken pot, which in turn is placed on a stone or other convenient base. As the potter works she rotates this. Sometimes a rude bearing of a stone or another small piece of pot is used so that the pot in the making can be turned quite rapidly. From such a simple beginning can be traced the potter's wheel, which, once it had attained a certain degree of excellence at a comparatively early period, has scarcely changed at all.

It would be interesting to narrow the subject even further and to trace the development of certain selected tools or household gear. Another example of pottery will make this point clear. The early Cypriot potters made certain vessels representing the human form. The head was represented by the lid, which doubtless often got broken or lost. Generations of potters, however, continued to put little daubs of clay on the front of the pot to represent the human breasts. The Cypriot potter when he makes this type of pot still puts on these daubs to-day. I once found in the market at Omdurman a pot which is before me as I write. This pot, although it is very much reduced in size, still resembles almost exactly the bronze age pot from Cyprus, but the two little daubs for the breasts have been replaced by a crescent with the horns pointing up. The potter who made it so far from its original home had little idea who first invented that shape.

Another profitable line of research is to trace and compare the various devices which are used with the same end in view. One of the most interesting examples of this type of study is the distribution of various instruments which are used for making fire. A lump of ore is simple, possibly the simplest. It is used in Tierra del Fuego, and was possibly so used by our ancestors at Cissbury. The flint and steel became very familiar to us during the war when matches were scarce. Besides its use in Europe it has a wide distribution, including its use in China and by the Malays.

In many parts of the world the friction of two pieces of wood together is used, an interesting method since Lucretius suggested that possibly man first learned the use of fire from the rubbing together of two tree branches during a storm. This " friction method " may be grouped into two classes. In one group the necessary friction is obtained by rubbing a piece of wood or cane on another piece, and in the other a stick is used as a drill and heat is generated in the drill hole. The first group may be subdivided as follows : in Polynesia, in the Solomon Islands and on the Upper Congo a stick is forced up and down a groove in a larger piece of wood and a piece of tinder is placed at the end of the groove and ultimately ignites. The Australian native saws grooves on his shield with his spear thrower. Among the Malays, in East Africa, and elsewhere, a strip of bamboo or other flexible cane is pulled along the underneath of a piece of wood which is usually held by the feet, the ends of the cane being held in each hand. The wood is usually split and a piece of tinder is placed in the split near where the cane is being sawn up and down.

The drilling method is very widely distributed. In Northern Africa, in Alaska, and in parts of South America, the drill is twirled between the palms of the hands. Among the Eskimo and other peoples a bow-drill is used. The most ingenious method we have already alluded to, namely, the production of fire by a fire-piston, a method which was in use in Europe as a scientific toy but which also occurs in South Eastern Asia.[1]

Yet another method remains whereby we may study primitive inventions. Instead of taking isolated examples either of crafts or of tools or weapons and comparing them with one another and tracing their evolution, we may study the arts of life in various types of society and may see how each society has developed its material culture. We should then see how man at various stages manages to live and, if possible, to live well.

I have adopted this last method in these pages because by this means it seems possible to estimate more exactly the relative importance of the various industries and of various tools within such industries. We can see thereby the part which each plays in contributing to human welfare and to human happiness. We see the implements of each craft not as museum specimens, dead and ready only for microscopic examination, but lying ready at hand for the craftsman to gain his daily bread or to triumph over his enemies.

By comparing the different geographic environment in which the various societies find themselves, we can estimate more exactly the real value of various inventions and the use that has been made of different opportunities. The effect of culture-contact can also be seen more accurately and we can estimate the

[1] The extensive collections in the Pitt-Rivers Museum in Oxford are arranged according to the evolutionary methods outlined in the preceding paragraphs. In common with many other graduates of the school of anthropology in Oxford, I must acknowledge the very great debt which I owe to the Curator, Mr. Henry Balfour, F.R.S., for his great and continued kindness, now extending over a good many years, in making me acquainted with the collections under his charge.

different degrees of originality or adaptability of peoples. Within the same group or tribe we can see how one industry reacts on another, both in primitive as well as in advanced societies, and the intimate part which handicraftsmanship plays in a primitive community.

CHAPTER II

THE DIVISION OF LABOUR

Chiefs and People, Man and Woman

IN the last chapter we considered the methods of study which we are to pursue; we must next inquire into the conditions which govern labour in a primitive community. Such people have far fewer tools than more advanced societies. The relationship between one craft and another must therefore necessarily be greater owing to the lack of specialization both of workmen and of implements. The savage is within limits " Jack of all trades." The long list of specialists which modern industrialism has introduced is unknown, but, as in our agricultural communities, one man is master of many crafts.

Even in the most primitive societies, however, there are specialists, who by their labour contribute to the general good rather than to their own direct advantage, although indirectly, of course, they benefit themselves. The principle of the " wages of supervision " is not unknown, or rather may be said to be very generally accepted, among savages. The headman of a tribe, in return for duties which are often of a very arduous nature, receives certain privileges and rewards. The chief's duties usually lie in other directions than those connected with the arts of life. Among warlike tribes he is concerned with the arts of war. Canon Roscoe has shown how among the Banyoro the whole well-being of the tribe, as represented by certain magico-religious functions, depend on the chief.

The position of the " medicine-man " when it does not coincide, as it often does, with that of the chief, is usually closely defined. He is a specialist who has certain duties for which he receives payment. If he neglects these duties this neglect is bitterly resented. On one occasion a Navajo woman complained to me that the tribal medicine-man had gone to a ceremony and that there was no one to cure her sick child, a grievance that led to many complaints among the people.

This principle of specialization due to leadership is, it must be supposed, one which has been recognized either explicitly or implicitly among the human race from very early times; indeed, it would appear to exist among animals which are gregarious. The position of the chief, however, will vary to a greater or lesser extent according to the organization of the society, and even according to its size. It is impossible therefore entirely to separate the study of the evolution of human arts from the study of the evolution of human society. The matter is further of considerable interest because many writers from the eighteenth century onwards, that is, since the time that the habits of primitive peoples began to be generally known, have continually suggested that the primitive organization of labour possesses advantages which have been lost in our subsequent evolution.

The original form of human society is difficult to estimate. Among many primitive communities inheritance takes place through the mother rather than the father, a custom that is known as " mother-right." In some cases mother-right is associated with certain material advantages to the women. Among the Hopi of Arizona the matrons control the property of the tribe, even going so far as to claim the women captured by the men in war. Among their near neighbours the Navajo, although kinship still follows the mother, the control of affairs is in the hands of the men.

Among most advanced societies kinship depends on the father rather than the mother, that is to say the children belong to the father's family and not to the mother's. The loose organization of so-called " group marriage," where several men have their wives in common, exists among some people but is an aberrant form at present, although some authorities believe that it is the original form of human marriage. It hardly affects our purpose.

Polyandry, where one woman has several legal husbands, and polygyny, where one man has several legal wives, also do not affect materially the arts of life. The difference of the position of the sexes is, however, important to this extent when we are considering the division of labour and the origin of invention, that it will often be found that the sexes, probably owing to physical differences, are apt to approach the same problem from a different angle.

In spite of these differences, however, the background of human society is the family which consists of a man, woman, or women, and children, and later, as society develops, of the stranger within the gates, the manservant, and the maidservant, who is usually in primitive society a secondary wife. The servants may be slave or free, but all of them work for the good of the family more or less in a specialized way. This family group usually forms a unit in a larger group, bound together either by real or fictitious consanguinity or by some other tie. Among most societies the government is in the hands of the men, although sometimes the woman is in command. The head of the house, and often the head of the group, is, normally, the owner of the property which belongs to his society, though his ownership is by no means so well defined as in advanced societies. He uses it as he thinks best for the welfare of the group.

The position of the head of a group or family in regard to the ownership of real property among a primitive people is very lucidly described by Rattray : " I have suggested how at a certain stage in the social evolution of the Ashanti a number of independent family groups chose the head of one of these groups to be head of the whole group. This head would already be the owner (in the very limited sense to be described later) of the lands of his own household or kindred group, but when he became head not only of his own group but of all the other groups composed of members of his own blood, and the title and powers of a chief came to be bestowed upon him, his piece of family land would come to be looked upon as an appurtenance of his chieftainship, and from merely being the family land of the family supplying the ruler would become by this association the nucleus of all stool land." [1]

This land, Rattray continues, came later to be augmented chiefly by conquest or by gift as an incident of conquest. Escheat and forfeiture were of rare occurrence, and purchase is of comparatively recent growth. Rattray defines ownership as follows : " The owner of a fee simple in Ashanti and the owner in England in

[1] R. S. Rattray, " Ashanti," p. 220.

the days of Edward I occupied a very different legal
position. It is necessary to remember that when we
speak of a chief, a head of a clan, the head of a family
group, as being the owners of land, we are dealing with
a stage of society in which individual ownership in
land was literally unknown. The Ashanti tenant in
fee simple neither had, nor has, anything like the full
enjoyment and control during his lifetime that the
'owner' had in England, even before the latter
gained the right to alienate. The Ashanti owner has
to account in full and be subject not only to the control
of counsellors, clansmen and family, but finally, as
already noted, in virtue of his spiritual trusteeship to
the dead. It may even be that the dead may return
and again claim their own."

The head of the house is the usual representative of
the family at any gathering of the group, although,
especially among societies who practise mother-right,
the men may merely occupy such a position owing to
their physical advantages. The position of men and
women in such societies is not dissimilar wherever these
societies exist. Rattray sums it extremely clearly
when he says : " But for these two facts (periodical
disability and inability to go to war) the Ashanti
woman, under a matrilineal system, would, I believe,
eclipse any man in importance. A king's son can
never be king, but the poorest woman of the royal
blood is the potential mother of a king. . . . Moreover, in olden times, when a chief had to be chosen it
was the queen-mother who had most to say in the
choice to be made. She would summon her clan mates,
male and female, and they would discuss the matter
apart from the sub-chiefs and elders belonging to other
clans." The position of the Hopi matrons in Arizona
is equally great, and in the olden days a man who

offended his wife was sent back to his mother without any redress except that his wife forfeited the heavy price which she had paid for him.

The specialization of chiefs, male or female, based partly on birth among some societies, partly on ability or on both, is of the greatest importance. The fundamental division of labour among primitive peoples is, however, based on sex. The subjugation of woman is rather a trait of barbarism than of savagery, and represents, paradoxical as it may appear, a comparatively high stage in development. To the savage it would seem a disgraceful thing for a woman to do man's work or for a man to do woman's work, and such actions would only be performed under the stress of direst necessity.

In most societies it is the duty of the man to provide the raw material on which the household subsists. The exceptions to this rule will be discussed at greater length later, as they are of the greatest importance. The rule holds good even among matrilineal societies, and is no doubt due to the fact that such labour makes a heavier demand on the physique and also necessitates the ability to hold oneself in readiness at any moment. It will be found that most of the inventions which are concerned with raw materials, with certain important exceptions, and also with war, were made by men. In hunting societies the man is the hunter, and he it is who travels unburdened, ready at any moment to attack such game as may cross his path.

A most instructive photograph referring to a higher stage of culture, that of the agriculturalist, not the hunter, is figured by Melland.[1] Here we see a party going on a visit, the man walks in front carrying a gun and spear, practically unencumbered, in order

[1] F. H. Melland, " In Witchbound Africa," facing p. 64.

that he may be free to protect his family in case of danger. The women say, " What would I do if we met a lion and my husband were carrying a load? " He is accompanied by an older child, who is big enough to run to his mother in case of danger but who needs the care that the man can give him. The woman in the picture is carrying some household gear and the baby. Among the same people, the Ba-Kaonde, it is worthy of mention that failure on the man's part to produce raw material, in this case to do garden work, is sufficient ground for divorce.

Among pastoral people the same duties are attached to the man. He it is who is ultimately responsible for the herds, though in many cases much of this duty is delegated to the children. Among the Navajo, in most of the settlements which I have visited, the care of the sheep seemed not to form part of the men's duties, though they cared for the herds of ponies. It would seem among pastoral people where many hands are required to look after the herds and where much of the work is light, that the men limit themselves to the care of those herds which wander far afield and need protection against wild beasts or their enemies. Owing to the nature of their occupation and the concentration of comparatively large numbers in a pastoral state, most of the men are fighters to a far greater degree than amongst hunters or agriculturalists, and the business of war often leads them far afield.

Among agriculturalists, although men often work in the fields in company with the women, the latter on the whole do so only at harvest and other times when additional labour is required, the greater part of the labour being in the hands of the men, even though, as I shall show later, there is evidence to suggest that the earliest agriculturalists were women. Among the

Ba-Kaonde[1] in the low-ground garden, in humus, the man cuts trees and fences where necessary, and in the high-ground gardening he cuts trees, collects and burns them, and both hoe the ground. In fact the man does the heavier work.

That this is not a mere isolated example, a proof can be cited from a people in a very different locality and condition of culture. In the Northern D'Entrecasteaux group of South East New Guinea, Jenness and Ballantyne write, " The youth directs his greatest energies to his garden . . . that he may support himself and the bride he is expected to take before long. The girl too plants and weeds her plot. Her brother or a near kinsman will do the heavy work for her, will fell the scrub and build a fence; *for this is the man's work always.*" (The italics are mine.) " In return she will do the women's work for him, and weed his garden in addition to her own. For almost the only man who weeds is the solitary widower; normally his wife or sister, his mother or daughter, does this for him, or some near kinsman of his own, or, in default of these, his wife's sister." [2]

Among the Hopi the significance of the work of the men in the fields of Indian corn is so great that the man knows, or knew in the old days, that he was going to be divorced if the woman neglected formally to thank him for his work in the fields on his return home for his meal.

Among all peoples, then, as a general rule, those crafts which require strength, travelling or uninterrupted labour are in the hands of the men. The spiritual welfare of the group, though that is outside

[1] Melland, loc. cit., p. 63.
[2] Jenness and Ballantyne, " The Northern D'Entrecasteaux," p. 94.

our present purpose, is usually in their hands, sometimes even among peoples where the women hold a very dominant position. Political power is usually, but by no means always, in the hands of the men.

It might perhaps be expected that man, responsible as he is for raw materials, would also be in charge of the water supply, a most important feature of savage life and one that often entails very hard and exacting labour. Women are, however, practically everywhere the water carriers.

There is a second class of raw materials for which woman is responsible, concerning which it will be necessary to make numerous references, namely, the collection of seeds among hunting peoples. Even those peoples who subsist almost entirely on animal food cannot exist entirely on this diet. The hunters are, however, fully employed often at long distances from their families in the pursuit of game. It falls to the women therefore to collect vegetable products, berries, seeds, leaves, and so on, with which to supplement their diet or to form a substitute for meat in times of scarcity. It would also appear that even under normal conditions the women and children seem to prefer a diet with more vegetable substances than the men.

Such seed-collecting is widely distributed among many primitive peoples living under conditions as different as the Eskimo, the Australian aborigines and the Bushmen of South Africa. At first it is undoubtedly a type of labour that may be considered entirely subsidiary. It has been suggested, however, that agriculture owes its inception to this occupation of the women. In its further development it became a trade, and, as I have already shown, domestic industries when they develop into trades normally pass from the men to the women. Among some peoples we find that a definite form of agriculture is practised by the women while the men are still hunters. If this theory is correct, humanity owes to the feminine sex the invention of a type of labour which has made all higher progress possible.

Apart from the invention of agriculture, it will be found that women's work is complementary to that of men, and, indeed, if what has been said above is correct, the invention of agriculture is due to the complementary nature of women's work. In the general economics of primitive labour woman plays a very important, if secondary, part. We are apt so often when we consider the history of labour to neglect her part until we find, under industrial conditions, that women's trades begin to grow.

Woman's place in a primitive community is a very definite one. So many of the early travellers report that the position of the women in certain tribes was that of drudges, a statement which disregards the particular duties of women in this stage of culture. Man is primarily the breadwinner, the provider of food in the widest sense. Woman is the distributor of loaves, that is, the purveyor of cooked food. She it is who is primarily responsible for our second great art of life, the preparation of food. She is intimately associated with the hearth and with fire. She is the symbol also of fertility, and without her influence the supplies of food may fail.

From this it follows that though most of the magico-religious duties are in the hands of the men, the keeping of the sacred fire is sometimes entrusted to special virgins, the most familiar example being that of the Vestal Virgins in Rome. The importance of this relationship of woman to fire and the preparation of food is illustrated by the marriage ceremonies among the Bakitara.[1] "At the end of the four days (after marriage) her parents sent a supply of food and her mother-in-law gave her a pot, water, and a stick for stirring the porridge, and explained to her, as if she were a child, how to use them and how to cook the food. The bridegroom provided a goat, and this meat was also cooked under the directions of the mother-in-law. A number of friends and relatives of both parties came together to eat the first meal the bride cooked and to visit her. . . . When the meal had been eaten, the wife went to the well with a small pot and brought water and a few sticks for the fire, thus completing the marriage ceremony."

Among the better-class Mongols of Inner Mongolia, a complimentary ceremony takes place which shows rather the function of the bridegroom and forms an interesting comment on the custom of the Bakitara. Here the bride's people gird the groom with a ceremonial bow to show that he is a warrior, and after the marriage has taken place the bride's father sends her three sheep, not as a due but to show that she is a person of independence, and that although it is not her function to provide meat yet she can do so if necessary.

Women only play a minor part in case of defence. They take a hand in dire need but otherwise they have no duties. Among some tribes, however, the Australian aborigines for example, it is their function to provide hair from which the bow strings are made.

The house is woman's especial province, but the building of a dwelling usually entails heavy labour, and therefore is man's work. Melland [2] clearly sums

---

[1] "The Bakitara," J. Roscoe, p. 280.   [2] Loc. cit.

the different duties of the sexes among the Ba-Kaonde. The man cuts the trees for the hut; builds it; thatches it; makes the door and bed.   The woman fetches the thatching grass; muds the walls and the floor.

Among the Hopi the house is very definitely the property of the women, and the ambition of every Hopi matron is to possess a dower house to which her daughter may bring her husband. The men do the heavy work in building. I was interested to find in certain Cypriot villages that some poor old women had no houses of their own. They explained to me that they were too poor to hire labour and had no man to do the heavy work for them. The felt for building the yurts among the Mongols is made by the men on horseback, for a Mongol man does every possible and impossible thing from the back of his pony. The women, however, are responsible for the periodic dismantling of the dwelling when a move is being made.

Once the house has been made, it becomes the especial province of the woman, and is sometimes her property. She stays at home and deals with the raw material provided by her husband. One matter alone does she provide, water, and this duty she delegates, if possible, to the slave. It is deeply significant in studying the arts of life to remember that the phrase " a hewer of wood and drawer of water " has passed into our language as a synonym for slave.

The household utensils are normally women's work. The ancient art of pottery therefore belongs to the women, though it has passed often to men in cases where pottery has ceased to be a household industry, but has become a means of winning the daily bread, and therefore a raw material. The getting of clay, which entails travelling and heavy work, is frequently in the hands of the men.

I once visited a village of Indians in Mexico, where potting had become the only industry in the village. But even here all the potters were women, and all the work of fetching and preparing the clay was in the hands of the men. In Mexico to-day, as a general rule, we can see the transference from women to men. In many or most villages, potting has become a craft and has ceased to be a purely domestic art. Some villages adhere to the old rule, in some the men help their wives in their spare time, and in others, in order to supply the regular demands of the local market, the women have handed over their implements to the men and confine themselves to household affairs.

In some countries several types of pottery will be found in use. Usually in this case the women make the more primitive pots and the men the more elaborate. Wheel-made pottery has been in use in Cyprus from very early times, yet in some villages the women make a very primitive type of mud pot without a wheel and bake it in the sun, not in a kiln as the men do. Near Kyoto, in Japan, there is a similar curious survival which must date from very early times. Here a few women make primitive dishes, shaping them on their elbows. These dishes are used in the Shinto temples, which possess a ritual notoriously archaistic, and the type of pottery these old women make without doubt recalls the old domestic pottery used long ago by the ancestors of the modern Japanese.

Grinding corn is notoriously a woman's occupation; possibly she invented the use of cereals. Among some peoples whose main subsistence depends on hunting, vegetable products are collected by the women. The making of most forms of primitive mills necessitates very hard labour, and they are therefore usually made by the men. In a market in Mexico, in those parts where Western influence is small, most of the trading is done by the women. The matates, mullers made of lava, objects which are so closely associated with the women that they might almost be taken as the symbol of femininity, are made and sold by the men, and the altercations which ensue between the women who have got to use them and the men who made them are often instructive.

The management of children is the affair of the women, and needs no further discussion. Little girls learn very soon to help their mothers in the house, and generally have a shorter childhood than their brothers. The making of clothes is also a feminine affair. Among the most primitive hunters this means practically the preparation of skins, and when we find to-day a little rounded scraper whose purpose was probably the removal of grease and flesh from the inside of skins, we may conjecture with some degree of reason that it formed part of the " work-basket " of some prehistoric lady. Among the Eskimo one of the chief duties of the women, and they begin the task early in life, is the chewing of skins to render them supple.

Weaving is a craft whose history is probably not dissimilar to that of pottery. Herodotus called attention to the fact that whereas in Greece it was the duty of the housewife to weave, in Egypt it was her husband who worked at the loom. It seems probable that early weaving was confined to the household, but that later it became commercialized, although among many people the women still weave. Among the Hopi the ceremonial weaving of a bride's marriage garment and her shroud, which is done before her marriage, is in the hands of the groom's uncles. The Navajo women, on the other hand, near neighbours, and ancient enemies of the Hopi, always weave while their husbands either look on or care for the flocks.

The introduction of slaves naturally materially affects women's work. In some cases they are made to produce raw materials, as among some of the African pastoral peoples, who make agriculturalists provide vegetable products for them. By far the most general type of slave, however, is the " house-thrall," often captured in war and therefore frequently of the feminine sex, whose menfolk have been killed because they are likely to be dangerous. Even at an early stage the slave born in captivity seems to have been found.

The introduction of slave labour materially lightens the drudgery of the womenfolk and helps to provide leisure which is so necessary for advance. There is evidence to suggest that many of the advances from barbarism to civilization were founded on slave labour. In general terms we may say that once a society living under primitive or comparatively primitive conditions is able to hand over the arts of life to slaves, great advances become possible.

There still remain some duties of women which appear early in human history. The earliest beast of burden is, as I have already hinted, the woman who carries the household gear while her husband travels unencumbered. Transportation remains an important office of the women so long as society is still in a nomadic state. We are apt to think of transport very largely in its industrial aspect. Among primitive peoples, however, it plays a very different rôle. Civilized communities for the most part are in the habit of bringing raw materials to their own doors, and transportation has therefore become an industry connected with man's duties. Primitive man, on the other hand, for the most part pursues his raw materials until he is sufficiently advanced to practise agriculture.

What has to be transported is for the most part therefore the household gear, for weapons must necessarily be carried by the man. I have already given an example of the duties of the woman on the trail. Among nomadic peoples this connexion of the woman with transport is further emphasized. It is they who pack up the tents and arrange the packing. Where carts exist, though the men may drive them, they exist for the benefit of the women. Their elaborate nature among the Mongols has been described by many of the earlier travellers. Not infrequently also, the connexion of women and transport is shown by the fact of their making the bands and the harness, which occurs in spite of the fact that the care of animals is in the hands of the men, who might naturally be expected therefore to make the harness.

Among nomadic peoples transport is an essential in some form or another. When the agricultural stage has been reached transportation takes on a different form. When the farmer goes on a visit, a frequent affair among the African peoples, the woman remains as the baggage animal. The man is the protector. Otherwise, however, the house and goods cease to be moved, and such developments as take place are more directly in the direction of heavy transport, and the carrying gradually becomes a trade and passes into the hands of specialized men.

Transport by water, however, proves an exception to our general dictum. That is seldom or never in the hands of the women. Jenness says that there are two things that every man can do in the D'Entrecasteaux

Archipelago—build a house and a canoe. Among the Eskimo, however, there are women's boats. These are specially used for travelling, and show the intimate connexion of women with transport for travelling. The boats of the men are essentially part of their hunting equipment. Among sea-faring peoples the responsibilities thrown on the women owing to this frequent divorce from transport are great. The boats, when they do not carry the household gear, divide the society into two, and the women who remain at home have perforce to do much of the hard work which is done normally by the men, and it has been said, though exceptions are so great that this matter may well be questioned, that the women in tribes whose methods of transport often carry them far from home are more independent and have a better position.

Finally, the relation of women to trade deserves attention. Among many peoples they represent the first type of alienable and individual property as opposed to the possessions of the group. It has been suggested above that group marriage is an abnormal and in some cases a late development, and although some peoples buy husbands the bride-price is an established institution and often causes considerable complications among those peoples who are passing from group to individual ownership.

In general terms it may be said that the purchasing of a wife plays an important part in the arts of life of primitive peoples, and I have given examples above of the position of a man who has no womenfolk to help him. The working power of a woman, in addition to her power of producing children, may be recognized as a definite commercial asset and one which possibly lies at the root of all commerce. Her value is in most cases great, and in order to obtain a wife a man must often devote considerable time to the production of necessaries by way of surplus to his own needs, a principle that is at the back of all trade.

Trading in various products is sometimes in the hands of men, sometimes in those of women, according to the organization of the society. The Hopi and the Navajo often trade together. A Navajo man brings up meat on a wagon to one of the Hopi pueblos. The Hopi women—it will be remembered that they are matrilineal—come forward with squashes, which they usually conceal until they have had a look at the meat. Then they bargain. It is reported that the women often get the best of the bargain. The Navajos therefore will sometimes bring their wives along to deal with the Hopi matrons, a comment on the shrewdness of the savage, in adapting himself to the habits of his customers. Trade always remains in a rather simple condition, although by no means unknown, among hunters and nomads, and usually the men who are brought more into contact with outsiders than the women do the trading, although it happens not infrequently that the objects of trade are manufactured by the women at home from the raw materials collected by the men.

CHAPTER III

THE PRINCIPAL TYPES OF HUMAN SOCIETIES

Hunters, Pastoral Nomads and Agriculturalists

IN the foregoing pages I have constantly referred to hunting, pastoral, and agricultural peoples, and it is often assumed that primitive man has passed through these three stages. The matter is, however, very complicated, and needs a further and more detailed treatment. The general classification is undoubtedly of great service, especially in studying the arts of life. It is based fundamentally on the food quest, which I have shown is the most important and the earliest of the arts of life. Man appears to have begun his corporate existence by passing through a stage which Milton has described as the " helpful experience of hunters, fowlers, and fishermen." This which seems to have been the earliest method of gaining food has never been abandoned even by the most advanced. Convenient as this term is as a label, it must be remembered that it only expresses half the truth.

Hunting represents the more spectacular side of the earliest forms of human culture. But it forms both a pastime and also an important part of the daily life of many peoples who are far further developed. Rattray, in describing a religious ceremony of a far more highly developed people, the Ashanti, quotes the following speech at a New Year ceremony : " Ta Kese of Aban, the cycle of the year has come round, therefore I and these my people hold this sheep which is from our hands and give it to you. May you stand behind us with a good standing. May you call upon all the spirits of plants and beasts that the bearers of children may be fruitful, and that the hunter who takes his gun to the forest may kill meat." This prayer shows that although the spirits of the plants take first place, as is but right among an agricultural people, yet the hunter has an important position in the community.

Among pastoral people who have abundant meat ready to hand it is not infrequently unusual to kill from the herds, and some of the cow people in Africa will hardly do so when on the verge of starvation. Some pastoral nomads on the other hand, even though they thus fear to harm their own herds, hunt the wild animals without any hesitation. The reindeer nomads of Northern Asia slaughter the wild herds almost indiscriminately.

Among the so-called hunters the products of the chase are by no means the only article of diet, though they naturally attract more attention. Vegetable products always play an important part, and the savage, like the leopard when the latter has no game, condescends to eat grubs and small rodents. Insects often form an important part of his diet, and where wild bees abound primitive man, in Africa the Bushman and in Asia the Vedda, to give only two examples, searches for honey, which he uses both in its native state and also as a means of making an intoxicating liquor.

Sollas,[1] in describing the diet of the Australian

[1] Sollas, " Ancient Hunters," p. 189.

aborigines, includes in their menu all the marsupials found in Australia, the dingo, the rat, all the birds and their eggs; reptiles, including lizards and frogs, are delicacies; fish are eaten; the insect world affords an important supply of food, especially grubs and the pupæ of ants (for which the Bushmen substitute termites). Sea food is an important article when available. " The number of plants which yield nourishment from one part or another is very great." It will be seen from this varied list that hunting, in spite of its importance, by no means forms the only means of subsistence.

Among some of the Arctic peoples, and indeed some of the pastoral peoples of America, meat is certainly the most important element in diet. This is probably due to the physiological necessity of a hard climate. It is of interest to note that the Navajo, who as far as I could see lived almost entirely on a diet of mutton, have linguistic affinities with the north. The parallel, however, must not be pressed too closely, as many objections can be found to the suggestion that their meat-eating propensities are the result of habits acquired in a different habitat.

The evidence of man's physique would also negative the idea that he ever was a hunter in the same sense that the carnivora are hunters. He has probably subsisted on a mixed diet from early times, with a varying proportion of meat according to the climate in which he lived and the game which was available.[1]

[1] The anthropological significance of vitamins has not yet, as far as I am aware, been worked out, but as in the following pages I shall have frequent occasion to refer to the various types of food which primitive man eats, a short discussion of the fundamental principles is necessary if we are to understand the basis of the earliest art of life. Briefly speaking, vitamins enable the body to make use of the

It is, however, convenient to describe as hunting tribes those peoples who do not regularly keep any domestic animals nor till the soil, even in the most primitive way, but this title must be used with very great reserve. The stage we describe as the hunting stage might perhaps be more exactly described as a " wild " or " collecting " stage, in which all the raw materials are the product of unaided nature, and in

various substances which are eaten. Without being themselves foods, the body nevertheless starves without them, and any primitive race, however abundant its diet, would necessarily fail if deprived of these substances. They are obtained either directly or indirectly from plants which alone seem able to synthetize them.

The details of their classification need not concern us here. The usual nomenclature divides them in vitamin A, B, and C. To secure a sufficient supply of B the diet must include a group of substances such as nuts, eggs, glandular organs such as the liver or kidneys, fresh fruit and green vegetables. A may be found in the four latter substances, and in milk butter and animal fats. C is to be found in fresh fruit and green vegetables. Climate, age and sex all are important factors in deciding how long the individual starved of these substances can remain in good health.

It is of importance to note that the vitamin content of the various foods may be very much impaired in various ways. Most of the modern methods of food preservation and of cooking affect them, but as these matters do not concern primitive man they can be omitted. Boiling or cooking only affects a part of the diet, but freezing, decomposition and drying have an effect. Although one of these factors may not seriously affect the food value, the combination of several may have an important result. Most primitive peoples it will be seen in the sequel no doubt get their full content of vitamins. Those who possibly may not are some of the dwellers in the tundra, but even in their case it is noticeable that in spite of a diet that is almost entirely animal they do mix some vegetables. Further, they seem to have a great craving for certain forms of food that are not likely to enter into even an experimental diet in a civilized laboratory, and they may thus make up for the deficiency that their diet seems to show. In other cases the diet of primitive man seems in many ways to coincide more exactly with the theoretical needs of vitamins than the diet of many civilized persons.

which man's part is limited to the collection of such materials.

Fishermen form an important and specialized group of the men who are dependent on the wild for their food, specialized because they are dependent on a particular location in order to carry on this method of livelihood. They are also often less nomadic because they are not bound to follow their quarry over big areas, although they often have seasonal migrations. Some of the maritime hunters in the far north, although they are dependent on the sea for a livelihood, are more hunters than fishermen, as they feed not on the cold-blooded inhabitants of the waters but on mammals such as the seal.

This stage of development is of particular interest to the student of early history, because it seems probable that our earliest ancestors lived in a similar state of culture. The parallel has been very clearly worked out by Professor Sollas in his book " Ancient Hunters." Various modern primitive tribes in the hunting stage are compared with palæolithic man. It is possible by this means to fill in many gaps which are left blank owing to the dearth of archæological knowledge. The difference in geographical conditions, however, under which primitive man in early Europe and, say, the Australians live, is apt to a certain extent to make the drawings of parallels a very difficult matter. For this reason in a later chapter I shall try and show how far we can trace the actual conditions under which man lived during the palæolithic period, and to see how they can be compared with those prevailing in various parts of the world to-day.

It seems probable that the earliest stage in human development was not dissimilar to that of some modern savages to-day, and that these wild men lived as do their modern representatives, mainly on meat in cold countries, and on meat supplemented with vegetables and other products in countries where game was less abundant or a vegetable diet more easily obtained. A further difficulty with which we have to contend is that, whereas early man was limited in his choice of habitation chiefly by natural causes, so many modern primitive peoples dwell in deserts and other inhospitable places, whither they have been driven by their more successful fellows. Conditions have profoundly modified their arts of life both by restricting the food supply and also by limiting the other materials which are needed to construct tools, weapons, houses and clothing.

Granting, however, these disadvantages and difficulties, it is possible by comparing the archæological material with the ethnographical to reconstruct to a large extent the arts of life of the early inhabitants of Europe, though hardly at present that of the other continents as we have insufficient material. We can also see to a very interesting extent how primitive man here differed from his modern representatives, and how far geographical conditions can modify primitive life.

Fortunately for the archæologist, not only do we find the remains of man himself and of his weapons, but also of the animals who were associated with him, and, in palæolithic times, we also have their portraits. In this way we have a valuable guide to the climate, for within wide boundaries certain types of animals are associated with certain types of climate and of geographical conditions; and also we have a guide to the animal food that man ate, and so a clue to the most important of the arts of life. In Cyprus in Bronze Age times, for example, it is reasonably certain that mutton was eaten. Several tombs belonging to that period, which I excavated at Lapithos, near Kyrenia, contained in what appeared to be food bowls, the shoulder blades of sheep, one of which appeared to be slightly burnt as though it had been roasted over an open fire. In a later chapter I shall therefore try and show what types of animals are associated with man not only to-day but also in early times.

It is difficult, except when dealing with recent peoples, to associate man with the vegetable products with which he was acquainted, owing to their perishable nature. Under certain conditions, however, plants may be preserved, and they often form a better guide to man's surroundings than animals. Animals can migrate and so avoid some seasonal changes, but plants, though many are world-wide in their distribution, are often singularly sensitive to their environment. Where we can associate early man and certain plants we are in a position to estimate more exactly his environment, though it is usually impossible to tell what part they played in his arts of life.

A great deal of man's development has probably not been the direct result of invention, but rather of what may be called culture-contact. By this is meant that one tribe has learned new methods at the hands of another, much in the same way that to-day most primitive people have learned at least a little of the use of metals, either from other tribes or directly or indirectly from Europeans.

There do seem to be certain cases where an independent invention has been made. Balfour has pointed out[1] that the distribution of the sawing method of making fire with a flexible piece of cane or other similar material occurs in three localities

[1] Journ. Roy. Anthrop. Instit., 1914, p. 32.

which are separated by great distances, the west of Africa, in one instance, very widely in the Malay Archipelago, and in Europe. In spite of wide culture-contacts, however, advances must have been made at various times. Some were no doubt gradual; others seem to deserve the definite name of inventions.

It would seem at first sight that the transition from the wild to a stage of life in which man to a certain extent made provision for the future must necessarily be a vast one. The change was, however, probably made so gradually that it almost escaped notice, so long did it take for one stage to be abandoned and the next to be definitely adopted. Apart from culture-contacts which have changed and are changing the life of primitive people profoundly to-day, the development from a wild life seems to have taken place in two directions, one pastoral and the other agricultural. Among some people it seems difficult not to suppose that the change took place almost in both directions at once.

The change to the pastoral life seems to have taken place in this way.[1] The hunter, it has been suggested, came to keep a few semi-domestic animals for use as decoys. There is nothing impossible in such a beginning, as many savages tame the young of animals, and the females, who would be most valuable for decoys, are usually less difficult to tame if caught young enough than the males.

Among the reindeer people it seems more than

[1] The question of the development from hunting to a nomadic stage has been discussed by Hatt, Mem. Amer. Anthrop. Ass., VI, 2 (1919), with special reference to the reindeer nomads. It seems not improbable that this thesis is also applicable, as he himself suggests, to other forms of pastoral nomadism. The reference to Langobardian laws quoted in the text is on his authority.

likely that the number of tame animals gradually increased and were used for special purposes until reindeer nomadism, as opposed to the old hunting nomadism, was established. It is of interest to note that the taming of these animals seems to be of comparatively recent origin, and that they have never become truly domestic. Hatt has pointed out that the association of man and the reindeer is to the mutual advantage of both. The animal gets a certain amount of protection, although he searches for his own food. He obtains salt and shelter. Man has the services of the animal. This apparently slender bond is sufficient to bind the reindeer to his keepers. The search for salt, especially in the form of human urine, seems to be the most important factor.

Most other animals which are kept by man have passed from the semi-wild stage and are dependent on man, not only for protection and shelter, but also for food. The ancient Langobardian and Alemannic laws suggest that the old Germans used the ox as a decoy for his wild brethren in the forests. This was in a later stage of development, and persisted down to the Middle Ages, but it certainly would seem to be a parallel to the case of the reindeer. A further practice which has persisted among many peoples of tying up the females of domestic animals in the forest during the rutting season in order to improve the strain, a practice also used by the reindeer nomads, seems to point in the same direction.

In some cases the domestic animals have developed into a sub-species different from the wild stock, but in many places the two are like one another. The little Mongol ponies are not very different from their wild brothers of the steppe. The progress from the semi-hunting to a pure pastoral state is naturally a long one, and it is possible to find many examples of an intermediate stage.

It will be sufficient here to outline the culture of the typical nomad of the steppes of Asia. Like the hunter he is a wanderer on the face of the earth. His food supply is, however, more abundant and ready to hand. It is dependent on the fruits of the earth, and in addition is singularly sensitive to climate. Man must therefore follow his herds in search of pasture and water, and also avoid the extremes of climate lest his herds should die. He cultivates, as Aristotle has described, " a migratory farm." He lives parasitically upon the animals. They supply him with food and with drink, with clothing and with building material. His bows may be made of sinew. He may use bone or horn for a variety of purposes. The herds are usually gregarious. It is this characteristic which has made them suitable for domestication.

A profound change therefore takes place not only in the arts of life but also in the whole organization of human society. Among the hunters, he travels fastest who travels alone, and the most successful hunter is he who has nobody to disturb the game. Among pastoral people there are, however, more opportunities for specialization. Even the children can look after the young of the herds, and the two live together in the utmost amity. The men ride far afield to distant pastures, to collect the herds that have wandered far. The women have at their disposal a greater variety of raw materials; they have also labour—the animals.

In certain directions, then, women's work develops enormously. Tents can be made from the hair or skin of the animals, and they can be more complicated because no longer must they be carried on the back. The gregarious nature of the life admits of a larger society, and children become of greater advantage. There is also at hand a form of food which is good for the children and the presence of which relieves the woman of giving suck to the children for as long a time, and therefore enables her to have a little more leisure, though the leisure of any primitive people is small enough.

The gregarious habit has the effect of making the pastoral nomads more capable in war. Their great mobility and their habits of organized warfare against wild beasts also probably adds to this condition. Whatever may be the cause, pastoral nomads have been some of the most warlike people in history, and often enslave people of a different stage of culture to provide some of the materials which they need but which are outside their own arts of life. In many parts of Africa, especially among some of pastoral Bantus, their agriculture is done by a race of helots who till the soil and provide for their masters. Similarly sometimes iron working is in the hands of slaves, for the pastoral nomad is usually singularly deficient in the arts.

There are a number of types of pastoral nomads whose habits differ considerably owing not only to the difference of climatic conditions but also on the type of animal which forms the bulk of their herds. De Préville, in his brilliant work " Les Sociétés Africaines," has divided up the cultural areas of the nomads in Africa according as to whether they are cow-men or camel-men and so on.

In Asia most of the pastoral people are dependent mainly on the horse, so typical of the steppes, and on the reindeer, who belongs to the Arctic tundra. Some people are, however, closely associated with the camel, the sheep and, in the high central plateau, the yak.

Although milk can be obtained from most domestic animals used by pastoral peoples, the essential dairy people are always those who keep various species of oxen.

It is of interest to note here that pastoral nomadism, once it has reached a certain stage, does not seem to be conducive to great advances. The pastoral peoples of the world, though they have been responsible for some of the most important facts in history, are apt to be cyclonic in their movements and conservative in their domestic life. Within limits, the larger the community the more successful it is. When, however, the herds grow too large, or the pasturage is too scanty, there is a quarrel "between Abraham's servants and Lot's servants," and the little community splits into two or more divisions and each goes their own way.

The nomad pastoral community is thus, especially in a big territory, capable of great expansion of a more rapid, if less permanent, character than any other type of community. The very nature of their methods of gaining a livelihood entail life in a boundless land, and their transport gives them an astonishing mobility.

The third type of society is that of the agriculturalist. Like the pastoral nomad, the agriculturalist probably represents an evolution from the primitive hunter. It is a type which has shown itself capable of greater things than the nomad though, or perhaps because, the lot of the primitive agriculturalist, except under special conditions, is a very hard one. The evolution of this type of society is one of special interest. We have seen above that one of the duties of the women in a hunting community is to collect such wild vegetables as are available. They also collect the seeds which are eaten. It is a very long step from the collection of wild seeds and the gathering of roots, leaves and fruits even to the most rudimentary type of agriculture.

Such an occupation is a very great advance on the collecting stage. It may be conveniently divided into several groups, partly on economic, partly on geographic grounds. If we adopt the latter the division will depend very largely on the type of crops grown; the economic division on the other hand has the advantage that it seems to correspond to certain definite stages in the evolution of labour.

A convenient division on this basis is that which has been generally adopted by the German ethnologists. The terms they use are " Hackbau " and " Ackerbau," which I shall for convenience use in this chapter. The divisions correspond roughly to our words horticulture and agriculture—the latter depends essentially on the use of domestic animals, the former on man's labour alone. That the division is not a mutually exclusive one is shown by the fact that most peoples who cultivate fields with their animals also cultivate gardens. The terms are, however, of great convenience, especially if it be clearly understood that when we say a people in the Hackbau or garden stage of culture we mean that they never use domestic animals for cultivation.

In the simplest form of Hackbau the earth is just scratched and the seeds planted. In temperate and sub-tropical lands many, if not most, of the staple vegetables are annuals and must be raised from seed. The beginnings of this type of agriculture may well have been not dissimilar to the method employed by Robinson Crusoe in raising his first crop. By chance seeds were shaken out on a piece of land where they could germinate comfortably. Such an accident probably happened many times before some primitive lady decided that she could lighten her labours by putting the seeds conveniently near at hand and thus ensuring a definite food supply. Bos[1] has suggested that at this stage there were in the same tribe two practically independent types of culture, the men being hunters and the women agriculturalists. Among many peoples the traditional connexion of the women with agriculture still survives. Among the tribes in the Northern Territories of the Gold Coast [2] planting is done by the women and children. A long pole with a paddle-like end, well planed down, is used to make the holes in which seeds are dropped, the holes being filled in with the foot.

The agricultural people of the Bakitara, who have been so carefully studied by Roscoe, may possibly have been affected by their pastoral masters, but here also the connexion of women and agriculture is very strongly emphasized. Among them the men cleared the ground, but " the whole care of the growing crop rested upon the wife, for the husband had work to do for the chief, who might make him build for him or herd his sheep or goats, or might send him to build for the king or to go out to war." [3] Among the same people Roscoe reports that men and women worked together at harvest time, although the actual reaping was done by the women. This latter statement is of great importance, suggesting as it does that the reaping was still, as it is among hunters, the privilege or the function of the women.

[1] " Archive internat. d'ethnog.," XI.
[2] Cardinall, " Natives of the Northern Territories of the Gold Coast."
[3] Roscoe, " The Bakitara," p. 202.

How early in human history this great discovery was made is at present uncertain; but it was certainly at the end of the palæolithic or the beginning of the neolithic period. It has been suggested with a considerable degree of probability that the soil readily polishes the points of implements that are used as mattocks, and that this accidental form of polish gave man the idea of using polished implements for other purposes.

The tilling of gardens seems to have been then originally an incidental form of labour, and, like most incidental forms of labour, in the hands of the women. When a stage of culture was reached in which horticulture became the principal means of securing food, it passed into the hands of the men in exactly the same way that so many other forms of labour, originally household duties, passed to the men.

Among many peoples we can still see the transitional stages, as in the examples which I have quoted from Rhodesia, where part of the garden work is still in the hands of the women but much has passed to the men. In many cases the women retain the duties of weeding, after planting perhaps the earliest of the garden arts. The transition is no doubt the easier, because as the art progresses the need for heavy and continuous labour becomes more and more urgent.

Under tropical conditions another and simpler form of gardening may be practised. Slips of plantain may be stuck in the ground by nomadic peoples, who will find a tree ready with a crop when they return to their old camping place. This method is one which was probably of early development among the dwellers in tropical forests where bananas naturally grow. Under the conditions which prevail in these forests the difficulty is not so much to make things grow as to put a check on the wild vegetation. This simple type of agriculture is one which might easily spring up in any forest.

Considerable stress has been laid by some authorities on the binding effect on human societies which even this type of human occupation has. The examples which I have quoted will show that on the whole among some peoples it may tend to bring the sexes into closer relationship with one another. Those societies which tend to seclude their women most are often herdsmen, although exceptions can always be found to this rule. The societies from which Islam sprang were pastoral nomads, not agriculturalists. Co-operative work among men is also a characteristic of even quite primitive agricultural societies. Jenness describes how among the natives of the D'Entrecasteaux group, " Several men stand in a row and drive their sticks into the ground, then with a united heave turn over one long sod of earth, leaving a continuous furrow." [1]

The most fully developed type of agriculture, Ackerbau, demands the assistance of domestic animals. The origin of this type has been variously discussed. It would seem to be quite a plausible theory to suggest that it also arose from a hunting stage, or from a stage in which the women practised agriculture and the men hunting. It is noticeable that animals are practically always men's work, and that therefore there would be no objection to the joint development of animal keeping and agriculture. It would need certain geographic conditions not favourable to the development of pastoral nomadism, and

[1] An excellent picture of this method is shown in his book which I have already quoted, opposite p. 124.

might, or might not, presuppose a definite stage of
" Ackerbau."

The most elaborate stage of agriculture is undoubtedly that which includes irrigation. Such
agriculture may be practised by peoples in an advanced
stage of development, and it is possible that those
primitive tribes who practise it, in the Philippines and
elsewhere, may have learned it from more advanced
neighbours. Elliot Smith would see in this the final
stage of invention which raised man above the plane
of savage life and banded him into a firm society.

The most important distinction, however, for our
purpose between the hunting and pastoral life and the
life of the agriculturalist is due to the fact that
both hunters and pastoral people tend to be nomadic.
For instance, though some of the Bahuma are said
by Roscoe to have settled habitations in a general way,
they did often wander up and down the country with
their herds. On the other hand, the agriculturalist,
except under the luxuriant conditions of a tropical
forest, must needs have a settled occupation if he is
to enjoy the fruits of his labours. He must build
a house to store up his harvest and his seed corn,
which needs a better protection from the weather
than when it is merely stored casually for food. He
has need of a variety of implements which he never
needed before if he is to be successful in gaining his
daily bread. It is therefore with the development of
agriculture that the higher stages of craftsmanship
really began.

Professor Elliot Smith in his book on the Ancient
Egyptians and elsewhere takes a view which at first
sight seems to be at variance with that expressed
above. He says (loc. cit., p. 2), " In the whole history
of mankind no single factor has had an influence

so great and so far reaching as the invention of the art of agriculture, which represents the beginning of real civilization. Former writers have claimed Babylonia, Syria, Phrygia, or some other locality as the home of agriculture, or put forward the view that the cultivation of the soil was devised independently by the people of all these places as well as of India, China, America, etc., when the pressure of hunger drove them to devise means of increasing their food supply. But it is now certain that such a reading of the early history of civilization is utterly false."

Elsewhere (Encyclopædia Britannica Suppl. Volume, s.v. " Anthropology ") he draws attention to the work of Professor Cherry, who has put forward much evidence to show that barley was first cultivated in the Nile valley, and that its cultivation elsewhere, that is in the Middle East, was only possible to people who were acquainted with the " natural conditions which the Egyptians had constantly before their eyes." It is in this cultivation of barley that Elliot Smith sees the beginnings of agriculture. He concludes, " The effect of the discovery of a means of securing a certain food supply capable of being stored . . . led for the first time in the world's history to a settled community."

While not denying the possibility of the first cultivation of barley in Egypt, which seems from the evidence put forward to be a very tenable hypothesis, it would appear from the evidence of cultural survivals among primitive peoples that the invention of agriculture was a very much slower process than that given. The steps can be traced so exactly among various primitive peoples, who, although they may use different forms of grains or plants, almost always

begin the same way, by collecting either seeds or
tubers, and later plant them, that it will be necessary
if we are to suppose that agriculture began in Egypt
to trace this method back.

We shall have to find Egyptians in the hunting
stage gathering roots, as the Bushmen do in other
parts of the same continent, and process till we reach
the stage when they can truly be called cultivators,
a condition which had already been reached by the
Proto-Egyptians who were already beyond the stage
of primitive man. It is the more remarkable, if the
Egyptians did invent agriculture, that they should
have been able to communicate it over most of the
world in the various stages through which it passed,
so that we have to-day survivals of all those stages.
The passage from simple agriculture to irrigation is
again hardly to be discovered by observing the
natural conditions. If that were so, the cultivation
of rice might have progressed more widely in Asia,
where the conditions prevailing near the mouths of
the tributary streams often closely approximates to
the irrigated fields.

The evidence of primitive peoples would rather
suggest that there was at one time a widely spread
culture where cultivation consisted in the sporadic
attempts of the women to cultivate while the men still
hunted. This condition spread by culture-contact at
an early date, and from it the great staple types of
cultivation arose—rice, the most important, barley,
wheat, maize, and to a lesser degree millet. That the
cultivation of a plant may have a rapid and wide
dispersion is shown by the part that maize plays
to-day in Asia.

Such a distribution of agriculture would date it in
a remoter period in the world's history than Elliot

Smith, if I understand him right, would suggest. It would also account for the facts which may be gleaned from the study of primitive peoples. At the same time it would make the use of the principal staple foods more intelligible. Otherwise, if agriculture begins with barley, why should other cereals be cultivated in places where barley will flourish? That barley itself may have been first cultivated in Egypt seems to follow from the evidence that has been put forward, but the stage where such advanced cultivation is associated with a settled community is beyond the scope of the student of purely primitive culture.

Elliot Smith's theory insists then rather on the actual place where agriculture first began than on the general classification and development of society, although he would see in the early agriculturalists of Europe faint copyists of the Egyptian splendour. From a different point of view the traditional classification of mankind into hunters, nomads and agriculturists has been assailed by Bos in the paper to which I have already alluded. His classification is based on rather different criteria, and he adds two further groups. Depending very largely on economic grounds for his classification, he considers that the lowest stage of mankind is that in which the chief industry consists in the collection of the products of nature, plants, animals and minerals.

The second stage is productive and includes the pastoral life as well as the agricultural. It will be seen that here what has been said above is in agreement with him, as I have tried to show that both pastoral habits and agriculture are the direct descendants of the hunting stage and belong as it were to the same generation of evolution.

Bos considers the third stage to be that in which

man is engaged in transforming raw materials into a finished product, and includes various crafts and dairy produce. His fourth stage is termed the industry of movement, an example of which he gives by suggesting trade.

Such a classification would appear at first sight to be an admirable way of explaining and grouping the various types of primitive labour, and indeed on certain grounds it is very convenient. It ignores, however, the evolutionary growth of human societies. It also disregards the fundamental law of classification in that it admits more than basis for subdividing the classes. It therefore tends to lead to confusion, because, as Bos himself admits, many tribes may come under two or more headings. Advanced societies practise all these methods of gaining food. Even people in an early stage of culture may have subsidiary methods of gaining their livelihood. The classification, then, that has been suggested in this chapter, with all its disadvantages seems at least for the present to be both the simplest and also the least unsatisfactory.

CHAPTER IV

THE CLASSIFICATION OF PRIMITIVE LABOUR

Food, Shelter, Clothing, Transport and Trade

WE have seen in the last chapter how primitive societies may be conveniently classified on the basis of the methods which they use to obtain their daily bread, and it has been shown that for the most part the average adult male is directly concerned in collecting the raw materials out of which food may be obtained. The collection of food is without any doubt the most important of the arts of life, and one which forms the basis of labour in any society. There are, however, other arts of life, even among the most primitive savages. We might almost say that it is this further development of labour which is one of the most marked points of difference between man and the lower animals. It will be our purpose in this chapter to examine and to attempt to classify these other arts of life and to see how the various types of primitive labour may be differentiated.

The preparation of food comes only second in importance to the actual collection of the raw material. It also holds a particular position in the study of archæology. Early food vessels are apt to be

55

destroyed because they are of a simple type and are made of perishable material. A very large number of primitive peoples are, however, in possession of certain types of pottery, an almost indestructible material and therefore of the greatest value to the archæologist.

From modern savages we can still reconstruct the method in which our remote ancestors probably prepared his food. The procedure, for instance, of the aboriginal Australians has been graphically described by Spencer and Gillen.[1] Making due allowance for a difference in geographical surroundings, this description would probably hold good for any people of very low culture. "We saw him (the Australian aboriginal) first of all capture his prey with his sharp-pointed wooden spear. Then, quite ignorant of metal knife, he had extracted the tendons, and cut its body open with a sharp stone flake, and had cooked it on a fire made by rubbing two pieces of wood, a hard and a soft one, on each other. . . . The intestines were handed to the women and children, who cooked them by means of rubbing them over and over in the hot sand and ashes of the camp fire. Two men had meanwhile scooped out a shallow hole with their digging sticks, just large enough to hold the body of the kangaroo, and had lighted a good-sized fire in it. After this had burned down and nothing was left save red hot ashes, the kangaroo was laid on the latter, some of which were piled over it, but not so as to cover it completely. The fur, which had been left on, was singed off or, at least, the greater part of it was, the skin serving to keep the juices within the body.

"After the animal had been cooked for an hour and

[1] "Across Australia," p. 130.

was still half raw, it was divided up by a man who used a sharp digging stick and aided his efforts with his teeth, and helped himself to special dainties as he went along. Those who found their portion was not sufficiently done rubbed it in hot ashes till it was cooked to their taste." Some hunting peoples, like the dwellers in the far north, prepare their food by boiling, not roasting. Most of them are not squeamish as to what they eat; in the north it is even eaten quite raw, but usually frozen. The preparation of food then at this stage is in a rudimentary condition. Nomadic pastoral people who are meat-eaters are usually equally deficient in methods of cooking. It may also be said to be characteristic of them, as of all nomads, to be deficient in vessels of any sort except where gourds are available. Birch-bark, bamboo, fish-skin and other materials are used according to the geographical situation, but pottery, although many tribes possess it, is probably borrowed from other tribes.

With the development of agriculture and a settled life, the preparation of food develops as one of the true arts of life. The invention of pottery dates back to the remote period and, although possibly some awkward sherds were made before man became an agriculturalist, in general its finer development did not come till man had a settled home; pottery is too brittle to be carried on a long trek. The numerous implements associated with the grinding of corn, querns, mullers and so on, although they may be used at an earlier stage, are usually too heavy to carry far, and their presence on a site usually indicates that the occupants of the site were comparatively or entirely settled in their habits.

The second great quest of human kind, finding

somewhere to live, is intimately associated both with the food quest and with geographical conditions. The hunter may live in a simple shelter in a tropical forest or in a limestone cave in Western Europe. He will use this shelter for one night or for a longer period, according to the amenities of the locality and the presence or absence of game. Where woman is the only beast of burden he cannot afford to have a very elaborate habitation. Many peoples in their seasonal migrations return to the same dwelling, so that this difficulty of transport is avoided. Cave shelters provide the most convenient form of home when available, and it is to the excavation of them that we owe much of our knowledge of primitive man in early times.

The pastoral nomad has transport at his disposal, and may often be described as a tent-possessing man. Not infrequently he inhabits plains or desert country, where he can find little or no natural shelter, and he is compelled to construct a movable home. The tents of the nomads have a family resemblance. They are often built of a framework of poles, which are fastened together and hoisted and then splayed out, the top being covered with felt or skins or birch-bark. This tent develops in various ways. It may become the tepee of the North American Indian, with the elaborate yet simple arrangement for letting out the smoke by ears, which catch the wind. It may become the warm and comfortable yurt of Central Asia, so easy to move and yet so efficient a shelter from the biting winds of the plains.

With the development of agriculture the art of architecture takes its place among the true arts of life. The contrast between nomadic and permanent dwellings are very striking when the two are seen side by side. The example I am going to give does not fall strictly within the limits of primitive peoples, but is so forcible that it deserves mention. In Inner Mongolia, in the district to the north of the Great Wall of China, the agricultural Chinese are slowly pushing forward into the cultivable part of Gobi, an area which was previously in possession of the pastoral Mongols. The latter live in villages of a semipermanent nature, usually in little subsidiary valleys. Their yurts can be easily dismantled in about half an hour, and there is little about the village that cannot be dismantled and removed. The most permanent structure is the sheepfold built of mud to keep out the wolves. The villages have nothing round them except the great heaps of dung which are used for fuel. Here the Mongols do not practise any agriculture, but depend entirely on their herds, buying what they need from the proceeds of the sale of their ponies.

From the south, on the other hand, the agricultural Chinese are slowly pressing forward. They do not travel far and at periodic intervals as do the Mongols. They are pushing forward their settlements into the virgin prairie at the rate of about a mile a year. Their habitations and villages are quite different, even though geographical conditions are the same. Their houses are made of mud. They are strongly built to withstand the very rigorous climate of the winters and the attacks of wild beasts or men. They have a high wall round them. It is possible to shut them up at night, and within the wall there is a courtyard where carts and animals can be kept. These houses can never be moved, and take much labour to construct. Such furnishings as they possess, and these are, it is true, not numerous, are heavy, the raised sleeping floor, the great stove and

bellows, so familiar in Chinese houses and so different
from the tiny dung stove of the nomads.

The surroundings of these little settlements are
also very different. Instead of the open prairie there
is frequently a patch of garden, and, in any case, near
at hand the fields of the cultivators can be seen. This
type of village is meant quite clearly to be a permanent
home. During the winter season the people are
ready to withstand the blizzards and the low temperature. Their type of house is suited to store up
provisions; they are no longer dependent on a
sensitive and moving herd for their living. It is
further of interest and value to notice that at present
they are slowly despoiling the nomads of their
pasturage, which they are converting into agricultural
land.

The house, then, will protect from the weather and
provide a place wherein to live. It will also in the
more advanced stages contain a means of storing
provisions. It will be movable or stable according to
the stage of society or the geographical conditions.
It is also necessary to find some protection from the
weather during walks abroad, especially if the climate
is rigorous.

There are some tribes, for instance the Fuegians,[1]
who in spite of a very severe climate wear practically
no clothing. Others living in a tropical forest require

---

[1] " Amongst these central tribes (of Tierra del Fuego) the
men generally have an otter skin, or some small scrap
about as large as a pocket handkerchief, which is barely
sufficient to cover their backs as low down as their loins
. . . but these Fuegians in the canoe were absolutely naked.
. . . A woman, who was suckling a recently born child,
came one day alongside the vessel, and remained there out
of pure curiosity, while the sleet fell and thawed on her
naked bosom and on the skin of her naked baby." Darwin,
" Voyage of the Beagle," p. 214, 1901 Edition.

little protection from the weather. It has been suggested that clothing arose not so much to protect the wearer from the weather, much less from an innate sense of propriety, as from a desire for ornament. There can be little doubt that the ornamental side of clothing plays an important part in its development and therefore is not our concern at this present juncture. The fact, however, that many of the Arctic tribes discard most, if not all, their clothing indoors, shows that at present, at any rate, they consider it to serve principally as a protection against the weather. Clothing therefore may be considered, at least in part, as one of the arts of life.

The type of clothing is closely related both to geographical conditions which limits the materials which can be used, and also to the state of society which controls the skill of the craftsman. The skins of animals have been used as an important article of clothing among many peoples from the most primitive hunters onwards, wherever fur-bearing animals have been available. Important as is the place of the reindeer in many arts of life in the far north, the value of his pelt is, next to the value of his flesh, the most important, both as a covering for the body and also for the tent.

Vegetable products have been used for making clothing from very early times, especially where good pelts were not to be obtained. In the Pacific area the cloth that is made out of vegetable fibre by a long and elaborate process shows what a people who, in many ways were not highly advanced, could do. Generally speaking, however, to make proper garments out of vegetable fibres needs a technique that is beyond primitive hunters who for the most part are dependent on skins.

The pastoral nomad, even without an elaborate technique, has at his disposal a rather wider range of materials than the hunter. He can use the skins and the wool from his flocks. He has greater abundance, and therefore normally possesses garments which are a better protection against the weather, although some of the primitive hunters of the far north have most complicated garments. The nomad also has not for the most part learned an advanced technique for the manufacture of clothing. It may be as much the objection to carrying extra weight which has been the deciding factor. The elaboration of the use both of wool and of cotton and other vegetable fibres is to be associated with a sedentary mode of life. Under these conditions the garment can be made at leisure and with machinery that need not be moved continuously.

Offence and defence forms a special branch of man's activities, and although in a sense it may be connected with the arts of life it falls into a special category, and therefore need not concern us here. It is sufficient to sum up the chief points briefly. First, it is often difficult to distinguish the weapons which a hunter uses to get his daily bread from those which he employs to defend himself against his enemies.

Secondly, for the most part, in a primitive stage of society man uses magic to kill his enemies, and the function of the medicine man includes protection of the group to which he belongs and the destruction of enemy groups. The magico-religious side of defence is so important as often to dwarf that side which belongs to the craftsman. The slaughter of large numbers is not the true function of savage war but is a later development,

Weapons have followed a special line of evolution, connected of course with the evolution of the other arts, but especially important in its own way. They have evolved partly in accordance with the material available, as have all other tools. The striking superiority of bronze over stone and of iron over bronze is perhaps more clearly to be demonstrated in weapons than in other instruments. Once the advantage of the new material is clearly shown it can be applied to many arts, but among primitive people time for the most part is of little account except in the case of defence against mortal foe, man or beast, and therefore in the art of defence the best material available will be used if possible.

Hunting, pastoral and agricultural societies do not for the most part differ in their weapons of defence. These instruments specialize as societies develop, but their function always remains the same, and many are extremely primitive even in their modern survivals. The mace is descended from the primitive club made out of the knobbed end of a tree stump. The stabbing spear, which has become a bayonet, has, it is true, passed through many stages, but the final result is not very different from its ancestor. The archæologist who has lived among modern warlike primitive peoples cannot but be struck, if he happens to open graves belonging to a people who resembled the former only in being warlike, by the great resemblance in form of the weapons of the two peoples, though one may use iron and the other bronze, and though all the other objects in the graves may be dissimilar.

Intimately connected with the arts of life, yet hardly forming one of them, may be grouped that type of craftsmanship which devotes itself to ornament and relaxation. Many, if not most weapons, have some touch in them which is unnecessary but which improves the appearance of the whole. Some of the finest stone implements are very clearly objects of beauty, and the conjecture that they seemed such to their makers is inevitable. Ornamentation needs leisure, but such an occupation as hunting allows the hunter periods when he has little to do, and therefore it would appear that he has an opportunity of which advantage is often taken to cultivate the æsthetic arts. Herdsmen frequently lavish considerable artistic care on their beasts.

Although the agriculturalist has from his settled manner of life more opportunities of cultivating the æsthetic arts, his time on the other hand is more fully occupied, except at certain periods of the year. It is also noticeable that most of the æsthetic crafts are in the hands of the men. Woman by her occupations has less leisure than man.

Intimately linked up with the more fundamental crafts, if they may so be called, are those connected with transport. I have already shown how the work of the sexes is divided on the subject of transport, the woman being the earliest beast of burden. At an early stage, however, man began to make use of animals as transport. The type of beast used is in close relation to the area in which man finds himself. The primitive hunters of the far north, even before they have reached a pastoral stage of development, make use of dogs for transport, a type that is limited to the northern part of the American continent, where it has been adopted by the white man, and to certain parts of Northern Asia.

Side by side with dogs in the north, reindeer are used by people who are still practically in the hunting stage of existence or, more accurately perhaps, in a transitional state between that of hunting nomads and pastoral nomads. Among most peoples the reindeer are used for traction, but among the Tungus they are ridden.[1] One of the most widely used of all baggage animals is the ox. He is used both as a pack animal and also for draught. Different species of oxen are used in different countries. The yak serves as a pack animal on the icy wind-swept passes of the Himalaya, the water-buffalo is used in the steaming savannas of Java.

Intimately connected as the various species of Bos are with the production of milk, their function as baggage animals must never be forgotten, and probably is the earliest use to which they were put. It is possible that dairy farming originated from the original taming of the beasts first in an early stage for decoys, and secondly, as it were incidentally out of transport, for milk, although it is interesting to note as a survival in the Mediterranean to-day that a distinction is made between " working " and " milch " cows. Some of the reindeer tribes do not milk their semi-wild herds, but the herdsmen occasionally take milk from the does by beating the udder and then sucking it, just as the fawns butt their mothers with their foreheads.

The horse is to-day one of the most widely used of transport animals. The remains of the bones of ponies in early Europe suggest that before he was domesticated the horse was eaten; possibly he was originally domesticated for food. Mares yield comparatively little milk, and though to-day the rich Mongols will have mares tied up outside their yurts,

---

[1] This reindeer culture in relation both to the arts of food getting and in relation to transport is discussed below, p. 169 ff.

the milk is used rather as a means of preparing koumiss and arrack than as a stable form of diet. The other important animals are the ass, also a native of the great Eurasiatic plains, and the camel. The milk of all these transport animals is used by various peoples.

While our evidence then shows that even hunters may keep domestic animals for transport, the use of large herds both for transport and also for their milk is essentially a matter which has been developed by nomadic peoples. They more than any one else have transport in a very developed form. The habit of packing beasts efficiently and rapidly needs long practice in the individual, and few primitive peoples have the opportunities for acquiring this skill except pastoral nomads.

The agriculturalist needs a different type of transport and draught animal from the nomad. The latter wants to move far and rapidly, the agriculturalist needs rather slow moving and heavy transport. Among many agricultural peoples practically no transport has ever been developed. This is especially true of Africa.

Those peoples who have succeeded in evolving a definite form of "ackerbau," as opposed to "hackbau," not infrequently have various types of transport. On one side this is intimately connected with the use of domestic animals to supplement the agricultural diet, a type of mixed farming, in fact, suggesting, as I have said, a development which is half-way between the pastoral nomad and the agriculturalist, and the other aspect of which is the use of animals purely for agricultural purposes. In this latter case they may be used either for pulling the plough or for true transport. It must be remembered that the keeping of cows even among advanced peoples does not necessarily imply dairy work. Although Bronze Age pottery in Cyprus, the so-called milk bowls and so on, suggests that the early people were pastoral, to-day the function of the cows is not to provide milk, except for the calves, but to pull the plough or the wain.

Transport by water is a very different problem, which has an intimate association with arts of life. It is closely connected with the food supply of many peoples. Geographical situation and climate both play an important part in the development of boats. We may also distinguish between transport by sea and by river, though naturally the two are related. As with weapons of war, boats have an evolution which is in a sense independent of the type of society of the users. Fishermen remain fishermen always, and though, at a primitive stage of development, all the tribe may devote their energies to fishing, even tribes who have not advanced to a high stage of culture may have certain members who are specialized hunters of fish.

The most primitive craft is made of a bundle of reeds, and is widely used to-day, for instance in Africa and elsewhere. The dug-out canoe is a common device where wood is abundant. The boat made of skins is a particularly interesting type which also has wide distribution and takes several forms. There is the classical craft of the Euphrates which relies for its buoyancy on inflated skins. Herodotus describes how these boats were floated down the river, and when the cargo that they carried had been sold the men returned home carrying the skins on the animals which had travelled down-stream on the boats. A second type of skin boat is of the coracle type, which still survives in Europe, but which has been highly developed by the Eskimo.

Among other specialized types of boats the outrigger canoe is one of the most worthy of mention. This elaborate canoe has made the passing of peoples over the vast area of the Pacific possible. It has bred a race of hardy fishermen, and has made seamanship an almost universal attribute of the Pacific. Fishing, then, and seamanship form the most important part of the labour of all coastal peoples, and survive amongst them when the society is passing through the various stages which we have discussed above.

The difference between transportation by sea and by land is that, exception made of a few adventurous spirits, the race of fishermen are not nomads. They return to their home port, they fish the same river. This sedentary nature of the fishermen as a society, as opposed to the wandering life which they lead individually, has an important effect on their arts of life. Like the agriculturalist, the fisherman, owing to his occupation and the nature of his transport, can afford to accumulate gear and at least a modicum of wealth. On the other hand, especially for primitive peoples, the sea, though inexhaustible, is a hard task-mistress, and the dwellers by northern seas, even though these may be the richest in the world, are often on the verge of starvation, especially when they are near enough to the Arctic to have to endure a frozen sea for much of the year.

Trade is not one of the arts of life in the strictest sense of the term, but it can hardly be omitted even from this brief survey, because of its intimate relation to primitive labour. Trade may be divided into several classes. It may be an incidental or a regular exchange between two peoples, the one habitually supplying that necessary which the other lacks, as the Maritime Chukchee purchase reindeer skins from the Reindeer Chukchee, or the negrilloes supplement the meagre diet of the equatorial forests by selling forest products to the agricultural negroes. In the Malay Peninsula the more primitive tribes traffic jungle produce with the Malays for luxuries which they have grown accustomed to. Skeat and Blagden are of opinion that the main difference between the extremely primitive and the more " tamed " tribes is very largely the result of the introduction of various non-jungle products by barter.

The earliest form of trade seems to have been that which has received the name of the " Silent Trade," which has attracted attention from early times and is described by Herodotus. This method of commerce usually seems to take place between two peoples who differ considerably in culture. The jungle people bring down the goods they desire to trade and set them in a prominent place, or it may be the traders belonging to a higher culture thus display their goods. The other side then come and inspect the objects for trade, whose owners have in the meanwhile withdrawn.

In some cases, where both sides have gained from experience a knowledge of each other's honesty, they give what they think fit. Where there is mutual distrust, they lay down beside the goods displayed the price they are prepared to pay, and again withdraw. The others then return, and if they are satisfied with the bargain they take the price away; if not they bargain by withdrawing certain objects. This " silent trade " is frequently in vogue where a timid jungle tribe is afraid to venture into the presence of a more advanced tribe.

Trade is thus associated with labour at a very early stage. Even the most primitive collectors of wild produce can enter into it. The only necessity is that one tribe is in possession of goods that the other lacks but desires. Barter by word of mouth is the direct outcome of such a form of trade.

The association of metals and trade is an important and early development. Metals, owing to their indestructible nature, their usefulness, and their comparative uniformity of quality and the ease with which they can be handled, pass readily from hand to hand, so that tribes unacquainted with their working often possess metal tools. Conversely, some of the metals that can be obtained in a raw state by primitive peoples often form a frequent and valued medium for barter.

There seems to be little doubt that metals were used for ornament long before they were used for making tools, and it has been suggested that malachite used as a face paint was the true herald of the Bronze Age, and so ultimately of all our industries which depend on the use of metals. Elliot Smith in the stimulating books which have been quoted above, and subsequently Perry, have suggested that the early spread of civilization was due to the search for metals on the part of certain enterprising prospectors from Egypt. They would see in the mining camp the true cause of the spread of civilization. There are many difficulties which must be overcome before these theories can be accepted *in toto*. To them, however, we owe a debt for having pointed out the importance of trade in spreading primitive culture and in changing the type of labour in which man is engaged. In any case it is difficult to exaggerate the part which is played by metals in stimulating trade and so inducing culture contact over a very wide area.

I have been dealing for the most part with trades in necessaries, although with the introduction of metals we are immediately faced with the problems of the so-called " luxury trades." There can be little doubt that luxury trades have the greatest influence on the development of culture. Certain arts which are first of all introduced to primitive man by trade as luxuries become subsequently necessaries, and by their means the general standard of living is raised.

It will be seen from the brief survey of the needs of man, which has formed the subject matter of the last four chapters, that the methods which man uses to meet these needs will depend mainly on two factors, first on the raw material available, and secondly on the degree of evolution which the society has reached and the extent to which labour has specialized.

There is also a third factor which is difficult to evaluate at present, namely, the physiological needs imposed by the climate in which man is living, a factor which may be justly considered as the converse of the first factor which has been detailed above. The combination of these three factors leaves an infinite variety of possibilities.

In the chapters which follow and form Part Two I have endeavoured to consider how far and in what ways man is affected by the presence of various raw materials, and also how far he reacts to the climate in which he is placed. We shall then have studied primitive labour from two aspects, first its general evolutionary development and gradual specialization, and secondly its relation to natural conditions.

In the third part I have endeavoured to work out

in greater detail certain types and stages of primitive labour. In some cases it will be found that I have returned to examples already quoted in this first part, but for the most part I have taken new examples.

I have only selected a very few of the possible examples because it seemed to me better to deal rather more fully with a few tribes than to accumulate numerous examples without any regard to detail. My choice of examples has been governed chiefly by three considerations. First I have laid stress, in dealing with the geographical as well as with the cultural aspects, on those peoples which seemed likely to throw most light on the early history of man, especially in Europe. Secondly, I have chosen peoples who seemed to be passing through a definite change in their mode of life, even though in many cases this transitional stage may have been of long duration.

Thirdly, wherever possible, and it is not as often as I could have wished, I have discussed those peoples with whom I have had personal contact, however summary. In many cases I have had few opportunities of observing the peoples at all closely, but I have felt that an insight, however imperfect, into the surroundings in which they live has made me better equipped to understand and balance the evidence which others, more fortunate, have collected.

PART II
NATURAL CONDITIONS OF LABOUR

CHAPTER V

THE INFLUENCE OF CLIMATE

Desert, Forest and Meadow

IN the previous chapters we have been considering the manner in which labour has become specialized among primitive peoples and the general direction which the evolution of labour has followed. During this inquiry our attention has always been focused primarily on man himself.

If we are, however, to understand the problem correctly, it is necessary, at least for a moment, to direct our attention elsewhere, and to examine not man but his surroundings in order that we may understand the more clearly what conditions are imposed on primitive labour by the outside influences of nature. This is all the more necessary because man, unlike the other animals, has been able, no doubt by the self-consciousness which he has developed, to triumph over nature and to a greater or lesser degree, even in primitive times, to free himself from many of the shackles which environment binds on every living organism.

While we find that many species of plants and animals, especially among the higher forms, have a comparatively limited range of habitat, man has succeeded more or less successfully in establishing himself to a greater or lesser extent in nearly every

75

quarter of the globe. The only regions where he may not be found are in high altitudes and in high latitudes, but even among the frozen snows of the Arctic the Eskimo succeed in eking out a precarious existence. There are tribes who live on the frozen tundra of Northern Asia, the Australian aborigines live in the burning wastes in the centre of the Australian continent, the pygmy negrilloes have found a home in the depths of African equatorial forests.

The great centres of civilization in Europe are sited on ground that for the most part was deciduous forest. Those of America are found where there was formerly either virgin forest or prairie. The old centres of civilization in Asia are more diverse in their siting; some lie ruined in what is now desert, but which once was fertile river-land, others are built on the loess of China; others again have sprung up under tropical conditions which seem at first sight most unfitted for the development of a great city.

It is possible to find certain parallel conditions of culture in widely divergent regions, for a people do not easily lose the habits of centuries, but the climatic factor, controlling as it does the food supply, plays a supremely important part in regulating man's labour and arts of life. A study therefore of modern geographical conditions is of the utmost importance for comparative purposes, presenting as it does a picture of the raw materials from which man must perforce draw his supplies for food and other necessaries of livelihood, and showing what was the base on which he had the opportunity of experimenting and using his inventive genius.

Both directly and indirectly, even to primitive man, the mineral resources of a country are very important. The presence or absence of flint in a particular locality no doubt profoundly modified its history in ancient times. Various kinds of clay have affected that ancient and widely distributed art, potting. Africa for the most part seems to have passed directly from a stone age to an iron without an intervening age of bronze, owing, no doubt, to the presence of easily workable iron, often actually on the surface.

It would be possible to multiply these examples at greater length, especially in relation to the part which mineral resources have played in trade from the earliest times to the present. But as man is dependent directly on plants and animals for his food, the biological aspect of geography is that to which the anthropologist must pay the greatest attention. It has been suggested by some writers, notably de Préville in his work " Les Sociétés Africaines," that the geographic factor is of supreme importance, and that it is possible to divide an area into geographic zones, each of which has a corresponding culture. Other writers again have been inclined to neglect geography and to draw parallels which are based mainly on cultural affinities.

Man, who takes the world for his home, has five main types of habitat in which he is compelled to live. He may dwell in forest, plain, or desert, on the mountains, or beside the sea or inland waters. The climate of the earth, however, varies according to the position which various spots occupy on the earth's surface. There are therefore hot and cold forests, hot and cold plains and so on.

Man's method of life will therefore vary according to two sets of conditions, first the climatic zone, and secondly the scenery with which he is surrounded. Mountains represent a special case. They tend, if they are large enough, to reproduce a series of climatic zones—forest, plain, and desert—as one ascends their slopes; they need therefore a special consideration. There is evidence, as will be shown later, that man in Western Europe was in primitive times compelled to submit to a changing series of climates which may now only be experienced in widely distant countries.

There is a considerable difference between the climate of countries which lie in the centre of continents and those which lie on the sea-shore, or in the immediate proximity of great masses of water. In general terms it may be said, however, that the succession of zones from north to south in the northern hemisphere is as follows : cold desert or tundra, pine followed by deciduous forest, cold plain or steppe, hot desert, warm plain (park-land or savanna), and tropical forest.

These zones are repeated to a lesser extent in the southern hemisphere, but the diminishing size of the land masses towards the south makes the formation of true tundra impossible; nor are all the zones present everywhere in the northern hemisphere. In some places, for instance, the tundra merges directly into steppe. In others the change from steppe to plain occurs without any desert belt. Sometimes one zone passes abruptly into another.

Two of the most striking examples I have seen of so rapid a change are the boundary between the desert and the sown in the Nile valley, and the divide above Kalgan in Northern China. In the former case the transition is from one of the richest to one of the barest parts of the earth's surface, in the latter to the north are the boundless rolling grass plains, to the south broken ranges and loess-covered valleys which have a different climate and culture from the plains only a few miles to the north. More often, however, the transition is slow, and the traveller realizes that almost unconsciously he has passed from one belt to another.

The northern limit of tundra is the polar sea. Its southern boundary coincides, in general terms, with the 50° F. isotherm in the hottest month, that is the northern limit of the forest belt. The distance between the northern and southern boundaries of the tundra varies considerably. The northern limit of trees is within the Arctic Circle in Western Europe, and in parts of North America, but much to the south in Siberia. The tundra is characterized by extreme dryness. There is little rain precipitation in winter, and the subsoil is permanently frozen. During the cold months, owing to the prevalence of high winds and small snowfall, the snow does not lie thickly on the ground. This fact is of the greatest importance to mankind; for the reindeer, on whom man depends very largely in that region for his means of subsistence, can feed by scraping away what little snow there is on the ground.

In the tundra there may be said to be only two seasons, summer and winter; the first is a sudden outbursting of all living things into a renewed life, and the latter a long dormant period of waiting till the rays of the sun are genial and warm again. The country is characterized by its barren monotony; there are no trees, only dwarf willows and stunted shrubs; apart from certain minor variations there is no reason why man should choose one part of this barren land more than another in which to place his habitation.

The reindeer depend for their food on mosses and lichens, and man follows his half-wild herds in search of pasture. In sheltered spots some berry-bearing shrubs grow—whortle-berries, cloud-berries,

crow-berries and cranberries, which are gathered by
the women in their season and form an important part
of the food supply. The animals most important for
our purpose, either because man is dependent on them
or because we find them in palæolithic deposits, are
the reindeer, the musk-ox, the lemming (*Myodes
torquatus*) and the Arctic hare. Another lemming,
Myodes lemmus, is also found, but does not extend so
far north. These animals are preyed upon by various
carnivorous animals, the wolf, the glutton, and the
Arctic fox, but only the latter is truly adapted for
tundra life. The polar bear does not occur in
palæolithic deposits, but he is the largest carnivorous
animal of the north to-day.

It has been stated that tundra life looks essentially
to the sea for food. This is eminently true of the
Eskimo living in the northern tundra to-day, but
there are other tribes who lead a nomadic existence
which is for the most part parasitic on the reindeer,
but also includes hunting and, where the rivers are
big, fishing. The animals we have mentioned above
which are common to the palæolithic and the modern
tundra can subsist on land. It is difficult with the
evidence before us at present to say how far palæolithic
man was a marine hunter. The sea animals, seal
and walrus, on which Eskimo life so much depends,
do not appear to be represented in ancient deposits.[1]
In palæolithic times, however, we seem to have had a
much bigger mammalian fauna, which suggests that
the resources of a modern tundra are rather less than
the tundra inhabited by primitive man.

To the south of the tundra there stretches a great
forest belt. It may be conveniently divided into two

---

[1] Some cave-drawings, however, are thought to represent
seals.

parts, the coniferous forest and the deciduous forest.
The conifers are adapted to a rigorous climate, and in
some parts of the world reach well within the Arctic
Circle. They are the home of the fur-bearing animals
which are so prized for their skins. Into this region
man comes as migrant; he does not seem to have
developed any form of society specially suited to such
an environment. When the climate of the tundra
becomes too severe he migrates with his animals into
the shelter of the forest. There, when the snow is
on the ground and the animals, weakened by the want
of food, are an easier prey, he sets his traps, and from
here he draws his supply of poles which cannot be
obtained on the tundra.

The region of deciduous forest, on the other hand,
has been the home of man for many generations. He
has modified its natural characteristics to such an
extent that it is often difficult to find out its original
character. Little of the virgin forest now remains,
for it is not so much the forest itself which is favourable to man, since he lives in the clearings rather than
in the woods. The conditions, however, which make
it possible for a deciduous forest to grow seem to be
ideal for man.

In its most luxuriant form such a forest consists of
trees alone; undergrowth in any thickness is only to
be found in the clearings and in open spaces, or in
land near streams which is unfavourable for the
growth of big timber. At the edge of the forest there
is often a thick vegetation. Closely associated with
the deciduous forest is meadow-land, which was in all
probability very characteristic of Europe in early
times. It represents a transition between forest and
steppe, and often contains patches of woodland. In
many cases there were in all likelihood meadows in

the large glades of the forest where the trees had been destroyed by fire, by heavy storms, or even by the clearings of primitive man himself. There is often meadow-land in the swamps near the stream or lakes. The forest contains trees which grow commonly in England to-day—the oak, the beech, the hornbeam, the ash, and in wet places the alder. There is a tendency in such forests, in distinction to what occurs in tropical forests, for trees of the same species to grow together.

Wild fruits grow in the open spaces, and even in the forest itself apples, pears, nuts, bullaces and sloes, cherries, blackberries, and the fruit of some of the forest trees—the oak, the beech and, in the north, the rowan—can be used for the food of man or the domestic animals. While not so suited to the growing of cereals on a large scale as the steppes, small clearings are protected from the wind and late frosts, and are admirably adapted for the beginnings of temperate agriculture of the small garden which includes a little patch of corn and such wild things as can be improved by cultivation. The moisture of the forest in winter and spring, and the comparative heat in summer, make the growing of plants not too difficult to be attempted, while the absence of a luxuriant vegetation gives the clearing a real value.

It is an interesting fact that the majority of our food plants grow best in a soil with an alkaline re-action. The plants which are native to a deciduous forest are on the best grown in a soil with an acid reaction. It seems probable therefore that the earliest cultivation was learned not in the forest clearings but on the steppes of the Eurasiatic continent. It is only in recent years that man has realized the possibilities connected with the cultivation of plants which have been used by him for food in a wild state ever since the neolithic age at the very least. We all eat the wild forest berries to-day. Only a very few of them are cultivated, though some of them which are form some of the most valuable of our food plants.

The woodland and meadow animals which are most closely bound up with the economy of man's life are not, as a rule, specially adapted for forest life, but are suitable rather to meadow-land. They penetrate into the forest chiefly to find shade in summer or to gain shelter in winter among the trees where the snow lies less heavily. Various species of deer are very typical of this type of country, although the species with the larger horns do not penetrate the close woodland unless compelled to do so by the extremity of the weather. They have always been hunted by man, but, although no species have become entirely domesticated, these animals have been on close terms with man. The forest produces a horse which is sturdier and less rapid than the pony of the steppes but which has been associated with man from early times. He is probably the ancestor of our Shire horses, Clydesdales and Percherons.

The wild cattle of the forest and meadow, the short and the long-horned ox, are the ancestors of our modern cattle. The bison of the plains has never been domesticated. The wild boar is a true forest animal; even as late as Domesday the value of the woodlands was reckoned by the number of swine which they could feed. For pure food value there is probably no other animal which has so well repaid man for the trouble that he spent on him as the pig. The eaters of flesh in deciduous forests have for the most part a wide range, and include those we have already met with in coniferous forests—the wolf, the fox and the bear; the last named animal is an important element of food among some of the forest peoples.

From this list of plants and animals it will be seen how dependent we are even to-day on the fauna and flora of these forests and meadows. The farm horse ploughs to-day the cleared land which used to be the forest where once his ancestors roamed. The cattle still feed in the meadows, now cleared and drained but still containing many of the wild grasses on which the old herds once fed. In our orchards we have the apple, the pear, the cherry, and the plum. But we have so profoundly modified the old conditions that it is often difficult to reconstruct the appearance of the forest. We know, however, that up to within comparatively recent times deciduous forests covered most of Western Europe. Where the forest was thick man could not find a home, but in the valley bottoms, on the open heaths and in clear spaces in the forest he invented and developed many of the arts of life to which we have now fallen heir.

The American woodlands have rather a different history. There is an absence of some of the animals which have proved most useful to man. These forests contain no horse, no ox. The most characteristic tree is the maple. Fur-bearing animals are numerous, and man did not develop before the coming of the settlers beyond the hunting stage.

South of the temperate forest the rainfall is insufficient for the growth of forest trees, but suited to the gramineæ. Here there is a zone which stretches right across Asia and which occurs in North America. It is usually known as the steppes or great grasslands. The Chinese call it by the more descriptive title of the country of the long grass. In this land the seasonal changes are very marked. In summer the great plains blossom with flowers innumerable, but the dry parching winds of autumn rattle through the dry stalks of the dead summer's vegetation. In winter the plains are desolate and monotonous beyond description.

I do not think that any one who has visited the great plains can fail to have been struck by their beauty. In places they are extremely flat, with long rolling downs, and little to break the sameness of the landscape. Here and there there are ranges of hills, some so low that they hardly seem to break the line of the horizon. Yet the plains have a charm all their own. At the right season the grass is full of flowers; the rolling downs with the long shadows of dusk or dawn upon them have a character that is to be found in no other landscape. The very absence of natural barriers gives a sense of freedom which cannot be felt elsewhere. At dawn in spring there is a nip in the air, for it freezes hard at night; the air is full of the songs of larks. There is nothing to interrupt the view; the very absence of contrasts makes for a beauty which is entirely absent from any other zone. In a forest you can see but a few yards, on the mountains the view is dazzling in its detail and its variety, but on the steppes, unless you look at the grass and the flowers at your feet, the view extends as far as the horizon—not very far if one's height above the earth's surface is only that of a horseman—and there are few or no details, everything is almost exactly alike.

Owing to the absence of shelter and the extreme climatic conditions, there are alternate periods of abundance and famine. The plants overcome this difficulty by many special provisions for a resting stage, the animals by migrations. It is necessary to pass rapidly from one feeding ground to another to avoid famine or the attacks of enemies. On the steppe man is dependent for the most part on animals, though he probably learned here first to cultivate grain for food. He too then learns to migrate swiftly, following green pastures. When the pasturage is good the flocks increase rapidly, and man adds to his numbers until there come to be too many to hold together in one society. The nomads then separate, each going a different way. In some cases under the control of a powerful leader the nomads sweep across a continent in exactly the same way that some of the steppe-dwelling rodents have been known to do.

The most marked feature of life, both among the plants and animals, is its social character. In a tropical forest we find an immense number of different species growing side by side. On the steppes, however, it is usual to find comparatively few species, but very great numbers of individuals belonging to the same species. Sometimes they grow together so prolifically that at last they invade other areas. It has happened that certain species of steppe fauna and flora have sometimes, aided by man, encroached on the forests. Where man's industry and skill in irrigation have overcome the natural dryness of the desert, they have settled here too, either as bidden or as unbidden guests.

The plants of the steppe which have been most useful to man directly are certain species of cereals which, originally cultivated probably on the edge of the steppe, are now grown over wide areas in the great plains and constitute the bulk of the foodstuffs of the world to-day. But the wild grasses also, which grow so abundantly on the plains, have been of the greatest service to mankind. They form the food of most of the domestic animals, either as pasture or in a later stage of development as a winter dry feed in the form of hay. All this vegetation is seasonal in its character. Though abundant and covering a wide area it possesses a food value only in bulk. It is not edible by man, who therefore, on the steppes, depends on animals in a domestic state, supplemented by hunting. Owing to dependence of these crops on the seasonal rainfall, a period of drought results in the failure of the harvest, and man must move to pastures new or starve. Some of the great movements of history have been traced by some observers to the failure of the rains in Central Asia and the consequent migration of the nomad herdsmen, a theory which it should be noted has by no means gained universal acceptance.

Many of the steppe animals have become the most intimate servants of man, others, without being domesticated, have been closely associated with him in ancient and in modern times. They include the saiga antelope, three species of horses, if we include the wild ass as a horse, and, where the steppe passes into desert, the Bactrian camel. The rodents include the suslik (*Spermophilus*), the marmots (*Arctomys*), the hamsters (*Oricetus*). These latter animals are almost certainly of steppe origin, but they have become attached to man like the domestic rat and mouse, and extend into Europe to-day.

It is not always certain, therefore, that when we find the hamster associated with man, that we can, unless there is further evidence, definitely assert that steppe conditions prevailed. Another genus associated with the steppes which has also been found with ancient remains is *Lagomys*. The eaters of flesh, except for a specialized cat and fox, have a wide range. The wolf ravages the sheep-folds, and is equally at home here and in the forests; even the tiger to-day extends into Siberia, though he is never to be found out on the open plains.

Of all these animals the horse is the one which seems to be most characteristic of the steppes. The nomad huntsman or shepherd lives in the saddle and is lost without his pony. He takes the camel long journeys to the north along the caravan routes, but I have not seen the camel far from well-trodden ways. The prairie itself is full of the burrows of the small rodents, and man to-day, like his far-off ancestors, traps the larger species for food.

The American prairies possessed in great abundance an animal of importance to man, the bison. In these plains the pastoral life so characteristic of the steppes of the old world was never developed. Man remained a hunter, and the periodic migration of the bison became an intimate part of his life. The white man introduced the horse and the sheep. To-day the Indian is restricted to the reservations, but the similarity of the life of the Navajo and the nomads of Asia, to which I shall have occasion to refer later, is a striking proof of the extraordinary suitability of the plains to the life of nomad herdsmen if only the right kind of domestic animal is available.

The transition from steppe to desert is familiar because it is described so frequently in the Old Testament. When spring comes the wilderness and the solitary place are glad, the desert rejoices and blossoms as a rose. The shepherd longs, when everything is parched and dry, for " the shadow of a great rock in a weary land." His ideal on a vast dry plain or on the rocky uplands is the rich deep meadows " beside still waters." In such a region there is a sufficient rainfall for the flocks and the herds, but such rainfall is apt to be precarious, and when it fails the herdsmen and his flocks die, for he has nowhere to fly to. The desert lies to the south; to the north the steppes suffer from the same drought, and have barely sufficient water for their own needs and cannot spare any for the wandering stranger.

In the desert itself there is insufficient rainfall to support even the most meagre vegetation. The air is too dry to allow the formation of any cloud to check the transpiration from the soil. The desert is often, if not usually, remarkable for its colouring. The surface is often very abrupt. It consists of rocky plateaux, sometimes small, sometimes of big area. These plateaux are often terraced, and are usually cut by deep valleys. There are areas which are covered only by sand, which, at least in some parts of the Sahara, is of a golden colour; in places it is stony. Plains and hills alternate; sometimes a wide area is covered with one or the other, or they pass rapidly from plain to hill. The rocks are often brown, sometimes black. The whole landscape has a dreary monotony, so that the traveller may often wonder how any man can live there. In places there are depressions with a kind of loamy deposit. These depressions, if they are sufficiently near the edge of the desert to receive an occasional shower, may sometimes be converted into pools, which, however, soon dry up, and the desert regains the entirely waterless appearance which is its true character.

In certain spots there are underground supplies of water which compensate for the lack of precipitation. In such oases dates or other edible plants grow freely, and, when irrigation is practised and the best use made of the available water supplies, the population may become very dense. Owing to the restricted area

competition with man has made wild life, especially
of the bigger animals, difficult. The big cats, however, live in some of the larger oases. Man has introduced some of the steppe animals. Owing to their
small size and dense population the oases are
particularly sensitive to any changes in climatic conditions. The slightest alteration of the water supply
forces the people to migrate; oases have therefore had
a most important effect on the grass-lands which
fringe the desert.

The climate of the oasis has changed, and the people
have then carried out into the open world a culture
which has developed under the sheltering and, at its
optimum, favouring conditions of a fortunate spot in
the desert. Cholnoky[1] is inclined to see in the
development of oasis culture the true cradle of
civilization.

Intimately associated with man both in the desert
and in the oasis is the camel, whose anatomical
structure is clearly adapted to life in true deserts.
Without this animal communication across deserts,
never easy, would often be practically impossible.

The American desert presents characters which
differ considerably from the deserts of the old world.
Perhaps the most striking difference is the absence of
the camel. In North America this area may be divided
into the country of the canyons which passes at
places into a semi-arid region and contains oases
which have developed their own characteristic culture,
and the highlands of Mexico which may perhaps be
more accurately described as half deserts. This arid
country has played an important part in human history,

[1] " The Ancient Desert Peoples of North America,"
Memorial Volume, Geographical Society of New York, 1915.
See also the same author's papers in the Geogr. Zeitsch., XV,
1909.

because it is in these regions that maize had its original home. In South America deserts are to be found both in the south and in the high regions of the cordilleras. These deserts have also been responsible for an indigenous culture, but owing to their altitude belong rather to the tundra class of desert, although they differ in many ways from that type of desert.

South of the desert and gradually passing into it as the great grass-lands pass into it in the north, there are in some parts of the world vast tracts of tropical park-land or " savannas." In the old world the steppe is the most characteristic feature of Asia, the savanna of Africa. In America both types of vegetation flourish over big areas.

Savanna regions differ from the steppes in possessing a greater wealth of detail than the great treeless plains. The climate is tropical, with alternating wet and dry seasons. Except on the borders of the desert, the rainfall is usually sufficient to support, if not trees, at least a tree-like growth of bush. These regions are often traversed by big rivers fed by tropical rains. Even in the barest parts of the savanna a " gallery forest " grows along the rivers, and every watercourse, even though it may contain water for only a small part of the year, is marked by trees. In some parts there are only trees in scattered groups at wide intervals, in others the bush is thick, thorny and difficult to penetrate.

The most typical plants are the various species of grasses, some of which grow to a considerable height and form thick cover for animals. Thorny acacias are very numerous. Along the watercourses often only a single row is found; elsewhere they form a thick bush taller than a man mounted on a camel. Some species of euphorbia, which has a characteristic xerophytic appearance like cacti, occur; palms occur sometimes, and the baobab tree is in places an important and conspicuous object of the landscape. Although not so markedly of social habit as the steppe plants, the vegetation of the savannas tends to be social in habit. Except among the larger carnivora, this is also a character of the savanna animals.

In general appearance savanna country in North Africa and in Asia are not dissimilar. Some parts of Ceylon, where the monsoon is insufficient for the formation of true tropical forest, has a marked similarity with parts of the Sudan, where the bush is merging into equatorial forest. Parts of Rajputana are very typical of the savanna as it merges into desert. The country is flat, sandy and covered with thorn. There is little undergrowth and little water. The crops depend entirely on the rains; if the latter fail so do the crops. To the man who does not like the scenery where the desert borders on the savanna, to ride through such country would be to suffer unending monotony. For myself the thorn scrub has a charm that is due, I think, largely to this very monotony. The dawn comes up not in the splendour that it does in desert or plain, but rather as the inevitable change between day and night. The shadows of the thorns grow shorter, you can see further into the bush, perhaps as far as the distant hills. As the traveller rides through such a land on his camel, he passes first through a bit of land in which there is only thorn scrub, then past a patch of cultivation, then more thorn, and sometimes a little village.

An Indian poet has written the couplet, " A hut of Ank (*calotropis*) with a fence of Fog (*calliogonum*), a cake of Bajra and a curry of Moth. Oh, Raja Man Singh, I have had enough of your Marwar." The calotropis is one of the most characteristic things of all the old-world semi-deserts. It is an evil plant with overgrown stems, which exude a foul juice, and large grey infrequent leathery leaves, and flowers whose petals are of a dirty pink in the centre and crimson lake at the edges. Even the goats and donkeys who grow fat on thorn will not touch it.

The American country of this type is different. The thorns have not the same characteristic umbrella shape. The most typical plants are the purple sage and the grease woods, which extend almost to the edge of the true desert. Beside the stream beds there are groups of cottonwood trees. In places at the right season there are flaming beds of composite flowers, very like our sunflower in appearance. Much of the country is at a high altitude, and here the desert cedar (*piñon*) grows in profusion, and provides wood and edible fruit. The bush is usually lower than the African bush, except among the piñons.

The savanna is the home of game animals. In the old days they were extremely plentiful in Africa, and included many species of antelope, and such characteristic animals as giraffes. The present surviving family of the rhinoceroses extends into the savannas, some of them being definitely adapted for browsing. The savanna animals have not, however, contributed any domestic forms, but they are important to man as a source of food; the gazelles are good eating, and are hunted by many tribes, the rhinoceros is eaten where his flesh can be obtained. There are species of pig which live in the savanna.

South of the savanna, in the northern hemisphere, bush gradually gives place to forest as the rainfall increases. The change is marked by a transitional belt where savanna trees grow. It would appear not improbable that the extent of forest in Africa was formerly greater than it is at present. Savanna with a sufficient rainfall is a convenient place for the dwelling of man. There is reason to believe that in places the clearings have encroached on the forest and introduced tropical park-land.

Over a great deal of Asia the rich, well-watered savanna forms the home of teeming millions. Here where the rainfall is often great the valleys are choked with a dense undergrowth, although trees are not very conspicuous, the most typical plant being the bamboo. Irrigation, which is a feature of agriculture in so many parts of the world, is here developed to its highest extent. The hillsides are terraced for rice-fields, and every stream is compelled to do duty by flooding the valleys. Such a country is very different from the dry savannas which I have previously described. Here there is water in plenty. The vegetation is luxuriant, even if normally rather low. Rice grows well, and the country supports a population which is extremely great.

From the rice culture of the wet tropical savannas there has developed a culture which is comparable to the culture that has grown out of the deciduous forests in Northern Europe. These tropical meadows are exactly comparable to the meadows which accompany the meadows of the deciduous forest. They have grown up sometimes in the open spaces of the forests, sometimes on the borders of the forests. They have enabled man to gather sufficient food to separate himself from his surroundings and to develop a material culture that is capable of extending beyond the geographic limits in which it originally grew. But just as the granary of the west must always be the great grass-lands, so the east depends for most of its

rice on the tropical savannas, although rice is grown
as far north as Hakodate, where in the winter the
irrigated terraces freeze.

Two animals more than any other which live in this
savanna are associated with man, although they are
really forest animals—the water-buffalo, who ploughs
the rice-fields, and the wild pig, who roots them up
and is eaten when man can encompass his capture.
The tiger has wide distribution throughout the whole
of this region in South-Eastern Asia. The animals
which are so often associated with man elsewhere—
the horse and the ass—are of comparatively rare occurrence. Man has either not found it worth while to
import them or has not succeeded in introducing a
strain which could stand the climate.

There are certain conditions in tropical forests which
make them of special importance to the student of
mankind, even though they throw little light on the
arts of life of primitive peoples. First, generally
speaking, the primates, to which natural order man
belongs, appear to be specially adapted to the life of
a tropical forest; the forms which have wandered from
this habitat are not numerous. It is true that man
probably came down from the trees and learned to
walk on the ground long ago, but his nearest relations,
the anthropoid apes, still live in tropical forests.
Secondly, the most primitive bones which can be
ascribed to man belong to this area. It is as yet
uncertain whether man in his most primitive form was
a dweller in these forests, and whether all invention
took its root therein or not.

An equatorial rain-forest is, on the whole, a very
disagreeable place. The vegetation is extremely
luxuriant, there seems to be a wealth of everything;
but, in spite of the absence of any appearance of famine,

the man who dwells therein is not infrequently on the
verge of starvation.   There is little animal life except
among the tree-tops, and the forest consists of two
worlds; there is an upper world, high in the air among
the summits of giant trees, a world full of life, to which
everything struggles, and a lower world, damp, dark
and full of decaying vegetable matter.   If you look at
a tropical forest from above it seems like a vivid green
carpet, whose surface is only broken by the gorgeous
colouring of the flowers and, if they can be seen, of
the birds.

Inside the forest itself there is no hint of this colouring.   The excessive moisture is a feature which cannot
but strike the observer.   Many, if not most, of the
tropical trees are very tall, and may send up a stem
which has no branches for a hundred feet or more.
Up in the air every branch is covered with a thick
growth of epiphytes, orchids and other plants, whose
flowers are often of the most striking character.   The
insects which visit them are hardly less brilliantly
coloured.   The seeds of these plants are dropped in
crevices by birds; their roots never reach the soil, but
obtain the moisture required for their existence either
from the water which always seems to be dripping from
the leaves, from the supersaturated air, or from the
damp crevices in the bark of the trees.   Wherever there
is sufficient space, giant creepers cling to the trees and
seem to disappear into the forest growth overhead.

In some places these creepers have become so inter-
laced with the topmost vegetation that they still remain
although the tree up which they climbed has fallen.
Normally, however, when a tree falls it brings its
attendant lianas down with it, and a gap is made, so
soon to be filled with a luxuriant vegetation, out of
which there eventually rises another great forest tree.

Few or none of the plants are of social habit. Although therefore the forest contains many plants which are edible, they are extremely difficult to find. We know from experience that where we find one hazel bush full of nuts there will probably be others; one blackberry bush does not grow alone, we find them all along a hedge. But in a tropical forest there is so much vegetation that even if we find one edible fruit tree we may starve before we find the next. The true forest dwellers are often driven to raiding the plots of their agricultural neighbours for food.

Where man has invaded the forest and established a system of cultivation, usually one that has been learned in the savanna, the conditions which make for the rapid growth of the wild plants help cultivation. It is merely necessary to scratch the ground, which has been previously burnt, and to put in slips of banana or yam, and these grow rapidly and produce abundant food. Once the cultivation is allowed to cease the wild jungle claims its own, and in two hundred years or so the forest has grown up to its original height, and shows no sign of the intrusion of the inventive trespasser who has dared to tamper with its sovereignty.

CHAPTER VI

THE INFLUENCE OF LOCALITY

Continents, Islands, Coasts, Rivers and Mountains

IN the last chapter we have been discussing the influence of climatic zones on human endeavour, with special reference to the food quest. If we are to understand primitive conditions of labour it is also necessary to weigh the influence of location. By this I mean the effect that a continental area, the sea coast, rivers and mountains play in shaping human destinies. Although during geological time profound changes may take place and the shape of continents be altered, although lofty mountains may be eroded and new ranges take their place, yet in relation to mankind these changes are extremely slow, and the mountains may be said to be immovable. Rivers and the coast, although they may change even within the memory of man, are a constant factor. In this they contrast strongly with the climate which, though it may be classified under certain broad headings, has daily and seasonal changes which profoundly modify men's actions and which affect his physique in a way which is yet to be explained.

Although the various factors to be dealt with in this chapter are not mutually exclusive, it is perhaps convenient to consider them separately for purposes of classification. We may divide the question of the effect of geographic location roughly into two main headings, —first the effect of land masses on man's arts, and secondly the effect of geographic physical features on men's arts, always remembering that climate is closely bound up with all these questions.

Land masses for our purpose may be divided into continents and islands, although some islands approach continents in their size and in their effect on mankind. Physical features may be divided into coasts, rivers and mountains. It must be remembered that in adopting this classification I am speaking not as a geographer but as a student of primitive culture. The biological effect of continental areas is to favour an evolution which is both absolutely and relatively rapid. The effect on mankind and his arts is similar. The most advanced cultures have developed on the Eurasiatic continent and have spread thus. Part of Africa is hardly separated from this great land mass, and has shared in its advances. The rest of Africa and the New World may be considered in the light of exceptions to this general dictum.

While no primitive culture has survived in Europe, and is only to be found sporadically in Asia, where it can often be accounted for by the effect of physical features or of climate, Africa, outside the Mediterranean area, and part of the Nile valley, which belongs culturally to the Mediterranean area, remained until very recently entirely primitive.

Much of the new world is still inhabited by primitive tribes, who are being rapidly driven from their old hunting grounds by the whites. A native culture was, it is true, developed, but its effect was purely local, and though it has made some important contributions to the material culture of the whole world by introducing the cultivation of maize, tobacco, quinine and cocoa, to name a few of the plants which we of the old world have taken over from the new, no really great advance ever was made, and the people never advanced beyond the limits of barbarism.

Man probably arrived late in this continent, but not too late to prevent the development of a definite physical type, from which it may possibly be inferred, although much evidence points in the other direction, that the physical type responds more readily to environment and develops more rapidly than culture. It may be that at one stage one develops more rapidly and that at another the other.

As a general rule we may say that large areas favour the increase of population, the intercommunication between various peoples, and the rapid advance of the arts of life. Islands on the other hand, even when they are of large size, restrict growth either of population or of culture. Except for certain restricted or unfavourable areas of continents, primitive man and primitive animals have a better chance of keeping their customs and characters in an insular position. On the other hand, owing to the protection afforded from other neighbours, the inhabitants of islands have a better chance of developing both a unique physical type and also a unique type of culture.

It must be remembered always that we are dealing with primitive man whose ocean travel, although great in distance, is restricted in occasion. Man has travelled very far, but he has not in early times often made such long journeys. The best example that we can find of such effects of island life is probably that of the Andamanese to-day, with their peculiar culture, and in modern times of the Tasmanians, who preserved till they were exterminated by the whites a culture which seemed to be paralleled only by the earliest examples of mankind from other parts of the world.

Australia by its size is almost a continental area, yet it has remained isolated so long that there survives in its aborigines another example of a type of people whose mode of life has been long abandoned by the rest of the world. Similarly until recently the Ainu in the island of Hokkaido preserved, and no doubt had developed in the past, a unique culture, whereas the neighbouring islands of Japan, by their closer touch with the continent, were able to make greater advances. When Japan, however, shut herself up within her island shores she developed from what she had learned from other peoples a culture which is so distinctly her own.

The very essence of islands is, however, the possession of a long coast-line; which pulls, as it were, in the other direction, more especially if a certain degree of culture is reached, and counteracts the isolating effects of islands. Even the wide wanderings of the Pacific peoples were unable, however, to raise them above a primitive state of life; yet the Malays, who started their advances only comparatively recently, were able very rapidly to throw over the primitive and hardly barbaric culture which is so prominent a feature of much of the area which we know by their name, and to borrow writings and the advanced arts of life from their continental neighbours.

Malta is an island whose history is particularly instructive in this direction. Of its very early history we know little or nothing; in chalcolithic times the island developed a special megalithic culture which has unique features. There can be little doubt that the isolated position which cut the island off from the struggles of the rest of the Mediterranean world allowed this advance to be made. Apart from this magnificent product of early art, Malta has little significance, and while the rest of the Mediterranean was contributing at various times and in various manners stones to the edifice on which our modern civilization is founded, Malta remained isolated and, it is curious to remark, is only referred to very occasionally by ancient authors.

Crete, on the other hand, developed, and taking advantage of its coast and the facilities offered by the sea, handed on a culture which was its own to the continent, which, as continental areas usually do, proved so efficient a scholar as eventually to destroy their *alma mater*. In the same way, but under very different circumstances, the island of Sumatra gave birth to the Malays, who borrowed the continental culture and then to their own advantage enforced their culture on the isolated islanders of the Archipelago.

We may sum up the effect of islands by saying that they contribute to the development of human arts of life in three ways. First, owing to their isolation they may lag behind the rest of the world, subsisting on the natural resources of their country and continuing in the state of culture which their ancestors had reached before they left the continental area. We may find, then, interesting examples of survivals among islanders in this stage, but few contributions to human progress. Secondly, islanders may, protected as they are from the strains and stresses of continental life, evolve a distinct and unique culture. This may be higher than the neighbouring areas, or may only be a particular adaptation to their environment. Thirdly, in the event of the island's unique culture being higher than that of the neighbouring continental area, they may hand it on and so contribute considerably to human welfare.

These general considerations deserve a more detailed exposition in dealing with human culture as a whole. In regard to the arts of life of particular peoples, however, the effect of physical features is more notice-able. Coastal peoples present features of special interest, some of which are allied to those we have dealt with already. A coast cannot be considered absolutely, but must be discussed in relation both to the hinterland and to the sea. In many cases the shore represents a narrow strip which communicates badly, if at all, with the country behind it. Under these circumstances man develops arts of life which are bound up with the sea.

The shell mounds which may be found in various parts of the world give clear evidence of the importance of sea food in early times. The description given by Darwin[1] of the Fuegians shows very clearly the effect of a coastal location on a primitive people. " At night five or six human beings, naked and scarcely protected from the wind and rain of this tempestuous climate, sleep on the wet ground, coiled up like animals. Whenever it is low water, winter or summer, night or day, they must rise to pick shell-fish from the rocks; and the women either dive to collect sea-eggs or sit patiently in their canoes, and with a baited hair line without any hook jerk out little fish. If a seal is killed, or the floating carcass of a putrid whale discovered, it is a feast, and such miserable food is assisted by a few tasteless berries and fungi. They often suffer from famine."

Such a condition approximates very closely in all probability to the life of any coast dwellers in a

[1] Voyage of the Beagle," p. 214, 1901 Edition.

rigorous climate. The food supply, however, of the sea is unlimited, and the evolution of coast dwellers who are dependent on the sea follows the line of an improvement in methods of catching fish. In whatever stage of culture, except the lowest, they have in the deep sea three methods of securing marine animals, by hook and line, by nets, although the net is first of all a river implement, and for the larger animals, and especially among mammals such as the seal, the harpoon.

Coast dwellers early develop, first, a settled home, which is enforced upon them by their mode of life, in contradistinction to the inland people who may be either nomadic or settled. Secondly, they develop the most efficient form of transportation. In early times and to-day the best way of travelling and of carrying goods and gear is by ship, whether that ship be an Eskimo Umiak, a dug-out canoe, or an oil-propelled liner. Owing to the seasonal changes of the sea, and the consequent risk of famine which all who depend on the sea must suffer from, trade becomes among the coastal people an important art of life.

Many inland dwellers are self-sufficing, or nearly so, as far as necessaries are concerned; they trade luxuries, but their food supply comes from themselves and is only supplemented from the outside either with delicacies or to make up for an occasional famine.

Without some supplemental source from which to draw the necessities of life, the coastal dwellers are always liable to die from famine owing to a succession of storms or other failure of the food supply. They are generally to be found either in a condition like that described by Darwin or they have taken advantage of their transportation to get into touch with other peoples and to supply by commerce what the sea fails to give them.

Elliot Smith would see in this development of trade the cause of the spreading of a world-wide culture, which he believes to be distributed over most of the globe. If his theories are correct, and at present the evidence he has collected does not seem sufficient, the importance of coastal peoples in spreading culture is much greater than has been hitherto realized. In any case, although many if not most cultures have a continental origin, except for a few prominent exceptions among the islands, the distribution, however, of the more advanced arts of life in each succeeding phase of human endeavour is almost entirely due to coastal peoples.

The coastal peoples with a hinterland which is productive are in a different situation. They look to the interior rather than the sea, and are therefore less liable to suffer from the periodic famines from which the pure fishermen must suffer. Among primitive peoples, however, the connection between the interior and the coast is usually not great. Sometimes, as I shall show in greater detail later, the coastal tribes may partake to a greater or lesser degree in the culture of the peoples of the interior.

This condition may be found among the Maritime Chukchee, most of whom possess reindeer. In this case, indeed, it is possible that the inland culture may have developed from the old coastal type by culture-contact. The people have turned away from the sea and its possibilities to the advantages of inland culture. The normal development from the coastal strip is then along other coasts across the sea, supplementing the rudimentary arts of life of the coasts by culture-contact with other peoples. In some cases, however, where the interior is fertile, the people will abandon the possibilities of communication by sea and look inland to carry on their life.

Rivers and inland waters are continuous with the sea, but from the point of view of the arts of life have certain important differences from the latter. Although river travel may at times be perilous, for the most part the navigation of rivers is simpler than that of the sea and probably began earlier. The rudest log suffices as an aid to cross many rivers. Transport up and down a river is simple and easier than along the coast. The river also, by its fertilizing properties, is favourable to the growth of food-supplying materials.

Where the forest is very dense the river provides the only way of moving from one spot to another. Where the ground is more open, not only are the banks of the river the most fertile spot but they are also the most easily accessible. The great river valleys of the world have therefore been the places where the population has become most abundant, and hence also where the arts of life have been most improved by the great competition. In short, it is there that the beginnings of civilization have taken place. The Nile, the Hwang Ho (Yellow River), the Tigris and the Euphrates have all been responsible for the beginnings of a departure from primitive modes of life.

Among purely primitive peoples rivers have a profound effect on the arts of life. In the first place they provide a constant supply of fish, varying according to the nature of the river. The fisher-folk on the river are therefore more in a position to adopt a settled mode of life rather than a nomadic one. Secondly, when an agricultural stage has been reached the river provides land of greater fertility than is to be found elsewhere. Most of the primitive peoples who live very largely on a vegetable diet will be found to vary such diet with fish if they happen to live near rivers.

Lastly, the rivers provide an avenue for trade and contact with the outside world. It will be seen in the sequel that most peoples other than the most primitive forest dwellers build their houses in the shelter of river valleys, owing, no doubt, partly to the advantages detailed above, and also to get over the difficulty of a water supply which is a prominent feature in savage life, where fetching water, if the wells are far away, takes up an undue part of the women's time and energy.

Speaking generally, however, it can hardly be said, at least among primitive tribes, that there are river peoples in the same way that there are maritime peoples. I should rather like to say that most primitive nations prefer if possible to have their settlements near rivers in order to enjoy the advantages which follow from such a riparian position. The river gives them an increased food supply and offers greater transport facilities. It does not, however, among the primitives, show a very definite type of culture.

Among civilized peoples, however, the reverse is true. A definite river culture has grown up in certain of the river valleys of the world, but these cultures have been, by the definition which I have given of civilization, clearly civilized and hence are beyond our present purpose. By these river cultures I mean those, for instance, of Mesopotamia and Egypt. It is possible that we may find that they developed from a primitive river culture, or we may find that, as elsewhere in the world, the older and more primitive culture was not riparian in its essentials, and that the river culture developed only in its later stages. The point will be found further discussed in the chapter dealing with life in tropical meadows.

Mountains play a very different part in the development of the arts of life. First it must be noted that a great part of any big mountain region must be classified as desert, uninhabited by man and, over a great part, never traversed by him in his primitive stage. A big mountain chain plays exactly the same part as deserts do in preventing culture-contact and the minglings of peoples. But in much the same way that deserts have their oases, mountains have their passes, and through these passes humanity and human methods of culture have poured. One of the most famous of such passes is the so-called Jungarian gate through which much of the culture contact between Europe and Asia has passed. The great boundary of the Himalayas has been one of the most difficult frontiers for man to pass, except at certain places in its length.

Although the sea divides, even primitive man can cross it, but some mountains are practically impassable on any large scale. In much the same way that islands have proved to be refuges where cultures have remained isolated, so often it happens that primitive peoples are driven from their own old territory and find a refuge from their enemies among the fastnesses, practically the desert-ways, of the mountains. A good example of the survival of older cultures of this type may be found in many parts of China. The various aboriginal tribes have been squeezed out of the lowlands, but have managed to continue their old methods of life, differing in greater or lesser degrees from those of the Chinese owing to the isolating effects of their surroundings.

The best example which I have had personal experience of the effect of altitude occurs in Mexico. The country is divided into three zones—the Tierra Caliente, the hot tropical land, the Tierra Templada, the temperate land, and the Tierra Fria, or cold land. The latter, which is on the plateau, is, in spite of its tropical situation, relatively cold. It is suited for the raising of cereal crops, especially màize. It was in these surroundings that the culture of the Aztecs appears to have grown up. The torrid country, on the other hand, differing from the plateau not in latitude but in altitude, has an entirely different flora; there is little possibility of the growth of crops like maize, and therefore the ordinary life of the people is very different, even though culture-contact is easy, and in many places the meeting-place between the climatic zones is surprizingly sharply defined. The primitive culture of the wet lowlands was most highly developed among the Mayas.

The contrast between the two cultures is most instructive for our present purpose. The staple food of both seems to have been maize. Maize is at home probably in semi-arid surroundings. It has been stated by Spinden that it probably could not be grown on the plateau without irrigation. It is, however, grown without irrigation but by being watered, as we water our gardens, by the Indians on the plateaux of Arizona to-day. In any case, it was grown on the plateau in the valley of Mexico and elsewhere, and ultimately, either by culture-contact or otherwise, a form of irrigation developed. The preparation of land in this area is comparatively easy, because the natural vegetation is small, and the principal difficulty that has to be overcome is the difficulty of water. This to a small extent is overcome by the plant itself, which, like many plants which live in arid country, is very deep rooting.

In mountainous areas, then, we are more likely to find the remains of primitive peoples when all traces of them have vanished from the plains. For similar reasons we are also liable in such surroundings to find sporadic traces of certain cultures rather than a continuous distribution, the surviving peoples representing broken fragments of a different culture from that of the surrounding lowlands. When the mountains are covered with dense forest or jungle this is still more likely to be the case. Some of the most primitive peoples of New Guinea, the Tapiro pygmies, have thus survived, a good example of the isolating effect of the combination of mountains and forest.

The climate of mountains has a very marked effect on the flora and fauna. The similarity of " alpine " plants, with a markedly discontinuous distribution, is a well-known fact. It is equally well known that the climatic zones which correspond to latitude are also equally marked in relation to latitude. At present, however, we rather lack clear data on the effect of altitude on the culture of mankind, except in so far as his food plants and animals are affected. Holland has drawn attention to the effect of the differences of altitude on two different branches of the Kulu Kanets of Lahoul, one of which lives down in the valley, and the other ten thousand feet on rugged slopes of the Himalaya.

In the lowlands the principal difficulty is the removal of the wild vegetation which grows very luxuriantly. Spinden suggests that the Maya culture is the direct outcome of the lowland environment of Central America. The staple food, however, here, as well as in the highlands, was maize, and it has been suggested that the plant was gradually acclimatized to the different conditions of the plains. In any case, it is interesting and not a little remarkable that, different as are the two environments, and indeed in many ways the two cultures, in both cases the staple food is maize. The Mayas seem also to have been hunters and trappers, no doubt owing to the wealth of animal life of the humid zone. Altitude in this case has not affected the food plant, although in its origin it came from the highlands.

We may find a fair parallel in the different kinds of rice grown in Asia, though here possibly there are more fundamental differences in culture. Here we find a distinction between the rice which is grown on the hills and the rice that is grown in the valleys. The difference is the more fundamental in this case because the hill rice is grown without irrigation, whereas normally the valley rice is irrigated.

In regions outside the tropics the difference between the mountain and the plain is the more accentuated because of the seasonal variation which necessitates a migration from the highlands in the winter, a migration which is practised by the Alpine peoples of Central Europe. This migration is exactly parallel to the migration of the northern tribes who spend the summer on the tundras but in the winter retreat to the shelter of the forest. The parallel is all the closer because in both cases the important feature of the migration is the herds. Among the northern people the migration is associated especially with the reindeer, among the Alpines with the cows.

In this way we can say that there are among mountain folk a nomadic almost tundra people, and that there do occur people practising at an altitude the desert culture that in other parts of the world is practised in the low-lying deserts. Further to the south, or lower on the mountains, we can also find the presence of a savanna culture.

The parallelism must, however, not be pressed too hard. In many cases the mountainous area has for other reasons not been favourable to the development of a definite culture, or the culture-contacts of the surrounding peoples have proved so strong that the mountaineers practise the culture of the plains, with such differences—the absence of fish, for instance—as are forced upon them by their surroundings. We are, however, other things being equal, more likely to find primitive peoples on the mountains than on the plains, owing to their more isolated and less congenial environment.

CHAPTER VII

NATURAL CONDITIONS IN PREHISTORIC TIMES

IN the last two chapters we have been considering the influence of climate and of geographical location on the material culture of present primitive peoples. These conditions are very different from those to which the earliest man was subjected, and therefore it is necessary briefly to discuss the various climates which have succeeded one another in Western Europe since man first began to live there. The changes which have taken place have been very great, and their causes have not yet been fully worked out. They may be divided into two groups; first, changes of climate, the details of which will be discussed later in this chapter; and secondly, changes in altitude with their corresponding effect on the size and shape of the habitable land masses.

Owing to the action of various erosive agents which are continually removing the surface of the land and ultimately carrying the greater part of the debris into the sea, the continents are being continually worn away. Deep beneath the earth, however, there appears to be a magma which is kept, most theories hold, in a continual condition of isostatic equilibrium. When therefore the debris from the continents is carried on

to the sea bottom, this later becomes heavier. The
magma is pressed towards the land area, which
consequently tends to be raised as the earth's crust
adjusts itself to the gradually changing conditions.   In
this way, in the course of very long periods, the most
profound changes may take place in the contours of
land surfaces.   Unfortunately it is not always possible
to reconstruct with any great degree of accuracy the
old land forms.

In this survey then, although we can take climate
into consideration, we must at least to a large extent
omit the influence of geographic location.   In this
way we shall no doubt fall short of the truth, and
our parallels will lack the exactness that could be
wished.   To-day we can hardly parallel exactly the
conditions which prevailed in Europe in early times.
We might turn to Siberia.   There we have grass-land,
meadow, forest and tundra.   But this area looks
towards the north, and to a lesser degree to the east,
not to the west, nor has it any mountains which can
be said to be the equivalent of the Alps or the
Scandinavian mountains, or a coast-line which can be
compared to that of Europe.

It must therefore be remembered that, though we
may conveniently view certain periods of palæolithic
culture as being characterized by a steppe or deciduous
forest type of climate, it can never have been exactly
the same as the steppe or deciduous forest which we
have discussed in explaining modern environmental
conditions; in just the same way that there are the
profoundest differences between the northern and the
southern hemispheres in their relation to the effect
of climate on man.

With this proviso, however, it is convenient to
orient the various types of ancient primitive man in

relation to his arts of life by exactly the same means which we have used in discussing his modern representatives, namely, by enumerating the various types of plants and animals with which he was brought into contact.

Under these circumstances I shall make no attempt to estimate an exact chronology or even to elaborate the various theories which have been propounded as to the stages through which the earth has passed. There is considerable difference of opinion as to which glaciations or interglacial periods coincided with the various stages of human culture. Some archæologists, for instance, would place the Chellean culture, which will be discussed in a later chapter, in the third interglacial period, others again suppose that both this and the succeeding culture period belong to a previous interglacial period.

Our present purpose is rather to consider the actual environmental conditions than the number of glaciations and their extent. It is therefore necessary to try and associate the fauna and the flora of each period with the implements, and to estimate the climate on the basis of these conditions, that is, to correlate the various cultures not so much with a certain glacial or interglacial period as with a certain type of climate. This will enable us to form an estimate of the actual temperature under which various types of man were living and to infer the environment in which he looked for his daily bread. We shall also be able to compare these forgotten arts of early man with those of modern primitive peoples.

In late Pliocene times the Mediterranean area nourished trees which are to-day typical of a tropical climate, including the sabal palm and the bamboo. The former is at present a typical equatorial forest plant in Central Florida. Further north in Central France the flora was similar to that of the middle United States, and contained species which grow in our gardens in Europe, such as the sumach and the tulip tree. Most of these trees have at present a warm temperate to sub-tropical range, although the sassafras, which also occurs in Central France at this time, has to-day a distribution from Florida to Canada.

Of this period we have at present but uncertain traces of man; the fauna too is unfamiliar, suggesting again a tropical climate, and characterized by such animals as the hippopotamus. It included some of the animals which we associate with the dry deserts of Africa, such as species of gazelles and antelopes. Most important of all, from the point of view of man, are the first true horses (*Equus stenonis*), elephants, one of which, *E. meridionalis,* is certainly associated with man later, and the ancestors of cattle (*Leptobos*). Towards the end of the Pliocene a change in climate altered the flora, and the trees which became dominant in Central France are those with which we are now familiar in Western Europe—the larch, the poplar, the willow, the beech and the oak. Simultaneously with the disappearance of the warmer flora we find that a change in the fauna was also taking place.

The first glacial period was accompanied by a great extension of the ice-sheet, especially in America. But in Europe the glaciers of the Alps descended so low as to imply that the snow-line must have descended about 4,000 feet. The flora includes the first arrival in Europe of the spruce fir (*abies*), and the musk ox is reported to have occurred in England at this time.

In the succeeding or first " interglacial " period, we find a flora which is familiar to us to-day. In Norfolk, for instance, we find the oak, beech, alder, willow, elm and birch, although the occurrence of some species seems to suggest a slightly warmer climate than at present. The fauna is, however, for the most part an unfamiliar one, and includes such animals as *Elephas meridionalis* (the Southern Mammoth), *Equus stenonis, Rhinoceros etruscus,* the giant beaver (*Trogontherium*), a bison (*Bison etruscus*), and an ox (*Bos primigenius*).

Among the larger beasts must be included the great sabre-toothed tiger, *Machærodus*. But in addition to these unfamiliar forms, we find a number of deer, some of which, such as the red deer and the roe-deer, have survived till to-day. Others again, the giant deer *Megaceros*), and the moose (*Alces latifrons*), have become extinct. We also have some typical forest-dwelling eaters of flesh, wolverine, bear, wolf, fox and marten. At this early stage we find, then, a mixture of two types of fauna, one not unfamiliar, the other of an eastern and different nature.

It has been suggested by Osborn that some of the latter had a woolly coat suited to a climate of warm summers and cold winters, but the presence of the fig suggests that the winters cannot have been very severe. That man was contemporary with this period is more and more probable as further evidence accumulates. At present, however, we can do little more than call the period " Eolithic "—the dawn of the Stone Age. We can find very little among modern survivals to parallel this remote period of time. North-Western Europe was probably rather warmer, and was clad in thick forests of a type not unfamiliar to us, and would be classified in our geographical scheme as warm temperate deciduous forest.

The next interglacial period is of the greatest importance to us, as at that period we have very definite

evidence of the existence of man.   Penck and Geikie
also, as we have previously shown, believe that the
remains of Chellean and pre-Chellean flint workings
near the Somme belong to this period.   Other writers,
such as Boule and Osborn, are more inclined to place
these workings at a later period.   There is no doubt,
however, that a human jaw found in the Mauer sands,
near Heidelberg, does belong to this time.

Evidence about man's industry must remain
uncertain.   At the beginning of this period the
temperature in the Alpine valleys seems to have been
about 4° Fahrenheit greater than it is at present, and
the snow-line about 1,000 feet higher.   The climate
was moist.   Later, however, although the temperature
continued to be high, the humidity was much less.

During the early stage the forests were for the most
part extremely like those of the present day, though
a few species occur which we should associate with a
warmer and moister climate.   But we find a number
of animals which the older geologists believed were
essentially of a tropical nature.   If we consider,
however, the evidence of the vegetation, and also the
fact that side by side with the animals which appear
to be associated with the tropics we have also traces
of a more northern fauna, it will appear not improbable
that the climate of Western Europe was actually only
more temperate than at present.   It must never be
forgotten that a very small drop in mean annual
temperature measured in degrees Fahrenheit makes a
great deal of difference to the plants and animals
living in that temperature.

The mammals that we actually find are *Elephas
meridionalis,* who is often associated with the greater
hippopotamus (*Hippopotamus major*), who survived
into the third interglacial epoch, but died out rather

earlier than *Elephas antiquus* and *Rhinoceros Merckii*, who first appear in the times we are discussing. In addition to these two latter animals we also find two distinctively African species, the African lion and the striped hyæna. To our minds the lion is a distinctly tropical beast, but there were lions even so far north as Thrace until well into historic times.

The old fauna that occurred in earlier times still survived. We still find sabre-tooth, the Etruscan rhinoceros, the Auvergnat bear and the great beaver *Trogontherium*. The deer that we previously met with survived, but *Bos primigenius* becomes more and more prominent, and *Bison priscus* is found. Among the smaller fauna are the wild cat, the wolf and the beaver. It was among animals such as these that the earliest remains of man have been found.

There is further evidence of a gradual lowering of temperature, marked by a southward extension of the reindeer, a typically northern animal, whose remains have actually been found above the stratum which contained the human jaw at Mauer.

This period was succeeded by a time of great dryness, with a climate of a steppe character, during which period the most ancient " loess " beds were laid down. These loess beds consist of dry dust driven by the wind, and sometimes they attain considerable thickness. Unfortunately we have at present no record of man at this time, and remains of animals have yet to be discovered.

Subsequent to the deposition of the loess deposits, the ice cap round the poles again increased. This third glaciation appears to have been even more extensive than the second in Northern Italy. In Britain, however, the icefields only extended into the Midlands, whereas in the previous glaciation the whole of Britain north of the Thames had been covered by ice. The climate in Southern England during the third period seems to have been cold and moist, the flora being that usually associated with an Arctic tundra.

Near Canstatt, Kohen believes that the woolly rhinoceros (*R. tichorhinus*) and the mammoth (*Elephas primigenius*) should be associated with this period. The matter remains as yet unproven, but whereas these animals disappear from Europe during the third interglacial period, they are typical of the fourth glacial period.

The next (third interglacial) period appears to have been similar in character to the previous interglacial times. We have again evidence of the same mammals, although *Rhinoceros etruscus* and sabre-tooth became more and more uncommon, and probably extinct. Dawkins, however, believes that the latter lingered on in Britain until post-glacial times.

If we follow Boule, Breuil, Osborn and others in opposition to Geikie and Penck, the earlier culture of Chelles and pre-Chelles belong to this period. For our purpose it is important not to emphasize so much which glaciation they followed as the fact that the industries represent in Western Europe a warm temperate climate.

During the period called "Acheulean," however, we find two types of climate, conveniently known as warm and cold Acheulean. The former is certainly of the interglacial type; the latter belongs to the pre-glaciation form of weather, in which the climate was that of cold, dry steppes. Contemporaneously with the changing of climates, accompanied by increase and decrease of glaciation, there took place a good deal of raising and lowering of the earth's actual surface, records of which occur in the terraces of various rivers in Europe.

These "terrace gravels," in which the remains of primitive handiwork have been found in great numbers, are of the utmost importance in dating the various forms of flint. They give us, however, little information of varying climatic conditions, except in so far as they indicate the size and swiftness of the streams at various times, and need not therefore detain us here.

These steppes were preceded by a cool temperate form of climate, but gradually the climate seems to have become colder and drier—in contrast to the cold, moist climate that we meet with in the immediate neighbourhood of glaciers. Correlated with this increasingly cold climate we find that the hippopotamus and the southern mammoth, *Elephas meridionalis,* disappear, but *Rhinoceros Merckii* and *Elephas antiquus* survive.

During this time it appears that Mousterian culture was developing, but it did not reach its full flower until the climate became more moist and typical glacial weather dominated Europe. This time marks the final disappearance of *Elephas antiquus* and *Rhinoceros Merckii*; their place was finally taken by a tundra flora, containing species we are accustomed to speak of as "Alpine," and a fauna associated with this type of flora. The woolly mammoth and woolly rhinoceros are the most remarkable and useful for dating finds, but the reindeer, which at this time spread widely over Western and Central Europe, gives a clearer idea of climatic conditions, as it is possible to study the distribution and conditions of life of this animal to-day.

Towards the end of Mousterian times the cold seems to have become even more intense; not only did the tundra mammals spread all over Europe, but some of the more definitely Arctic species, such as the musk-ox and the banded lemming (*Myodes torquatus*) and Obi lemming (*Myodes obensis*), migrated into Europe. The larger carnivora, the lion and hyæna, survived in the form of the cave lion and cave hyæna. These animals are only sub-species of the lion and spotted hyæna we know to-day, but their presence is in no way indicative of climate, as we know that the tiger and the leopard have in conjunction with other flesh-eating mammals a wide geographic range in modern times, their coats becoming thicker in order to withstand the cold.

In the valley of the Thames the Arctic willow (*Salix polaris*) and the dwarf birch (*Betula glandulosa*) flourished, pointing to an extremely rigorous climate. The reindeer, lemmings, and the two plants we have mentioned, suggest that at this time the seasonal character of the climate was of great anthropological importance. As we shall have occasion to show later, modern polar peoples live an entirely different life in the winter and summer, and there are parts of Siberia where the winter and summer isotherms are immensely separated. It is not improbable that similar conditions may have existed at this time.

The Mousterian culture probably died out as the final stage of the glaciation took place. The Arctic fauna, such as the lemmings, continued in Aurignacian times, but they were gradually supplanted, first by tundra and later by steppe animals, but during Aurignacian times the former certainly predominated. They included such species as the reindeer, woolly mammoth and woolly rhinoceros, the Arctic hare and the Arctic fox. But it is of importance to note that the musk-ox is rare, and that the wild horse of the steppes and the Central Asiatic ass are present. Woodland animals such as red deer, roe-deer, wolf, lynx and weasel are found. The giant deer seems to have died out in early Aurignacian times. Among the wild cattle the bison and the aurochs are found. It will be seen from this that the general type of fauna is tundra; one or two steppe animals only occur.

The climate in Solutrean times is at present rather uncertain. In South-Western France it has been suggested that a dry, cold, continental climate existed of a steppe character. In the Dordogne the most characteristic animal was the reindeer, and the Obi lemming occurs, but contemporary with these and the mammoth we have a typical north temperate European forest fauna, suggesting that France climatically represented a borderland between tundra and deciduous forest, rather than steppe as suggested by Osborn, as the reindeer and the lemming occur north but not south of the great forest belt to-day. As we shall see, however, later, the Solutrean period presents many difficulties, and any discussion of climatic conditions must be purely tentative.

The Magdalenian period certainly represents a change from a cold, dry climate to a moister type. The snow-line in the Alps descended nearly three thousand feet, and the Arctic lemmings returned in large numbers. The epoch has been divided into three periods, the first of which has been termed by Geikie in Scotland the fifth glacial epoch. At this time there was certainly increased glaciation in the Alps, and the return of a typical cold tundra fauna; in the middle Magdalenian period these cold-lovers gave place to a typical steppe fauna, suggesting a slight elevation of temperature, but not of moisture; finally, at the end of Magdalenian times, the climate was sufficiently

warm and moist to support a deciduous forest in
Western Europe of the same type as the great
Hercynian forest of Central Europe in classical
times.

The plants and animals which support these con-
clusions are in the first period. We find in the
Northern Alps polar willows, dwarf birches and reindeer moss. Among animals we have banded lemmings,
Obi lemmings, Arctic hare, mammoth, ermine and
reindeer. In fact, as Osborn says, we have almost
all the tundra fauna except the polar bear, and he is
only a summer migrant into the tundra.

The flora of the second period appears to have
consisted of grasses combined with temperate forest
trees, and the fauna to have represented an even
mixture of steppe and tundra forms, including the
Saiga antelope—which may have occurred in England
in Aurignacian times—the suslik, the steppe hamster,
the great jerboa, side by side with the bison, the urus
and the reindeer. In the final Magdalenian period
only a few of the steppe animals remain, but we have
such deciduous forest animals as the squirrel, ermine
and marten. Reindeer still occur, but at some stations,
such as Mas d'Azil, their remains become rare.

The oscillations of the ice-sheet at this period are
of great interest, and have been very carefully studied
in Scandinavia, where De Geer, working on the annual
deposit of the melting glaciers, has attempted to
establish an absolute chronology. We have already
seen that during the Magdalenian period we have a
cold moist climate with a much lower snow-line. The
movements in the north are not absolutely synchronous
with those in the Alps, and the Baltic region was, of
course, colder than Central Europe.

In Denmark the succession seems to have been of

this nature. The last ice-sheet covered most of Scandinavia and Schleswig, but parts of Denmark and Southern Sweden were not glaciated. This period was succeeded by the so-called Yoldia period. This name is taken from a characteristic mollusc which flourished in the Baltic at the time. This form is essentially Arctic, and the sea was probably always near freezing point. The land plants suggest a cold tundra. The flora is usually called the " Dryas flora," from the typical species *Dryas octopetala*, a flower which is found in Britain to-day growing on mountains, although it is a truly Arctic species. It is not improbable that the summers were quite hot.

At the end of the Yoldia period, owing to the raising of the land, the Baltic became a land-locked lake. It is usually known by the name of the Ancylus Sea from the typical species of mollusc. During this time the Arctic flora retreated. Their place was taken in Denmark first by willows, aspens and other poplars, and later by pines and alders. It seems probable that the settlements at Maglemose, where large shell heaps have been found, took place at this time.

In Western Europe where conditions were somewhat different the Azilian-Tardenoisian culture was probably at its zenith. Here a typical true forest fauna is dominant; the reindeer has disappeared, but the red deer, the roe-deer, the wild boar, beaver and brown bear are found.

This period was followed by a depression of the land surface in the north. The seas were probably warmer and the land temperature about 4½° F. warmer than at present in the summer. Oaks took the place of pine, and they again were succeeded by beeches. This period, which is known in the north as the Littorina period, is marked by the spread of the shell heaps. It corresponds to the Campignian period further to the south.

While these changes were taking place in Northern Europe, the westerly part of the Continent was also changing, and I have indicated above how the periods may be synchronized. The fundamental change which occurred here was due to the substitution of oceanic for continental conditions. The warm south-westerly winds which are such a feature of our climate to-day had begun to affect that part which we know as Western Europe to-day. In earlier times they had expended their warmth and moisture on lands which are now buried beneath the sea. The moose still survived in the Pyrenees and the reindeer in the north of Central Europe, but he still survived there till mediaeval times, although in Tardenoisian his distribution seems to have been wider, for his bones and those of other Arctic mammals are found in Tardenoisian hearths as far west as Belgium.

To the south, however, in the Dordogne and the Pyrenees, the lion and the Arctic wolverine are the only exceptions to what may be described as a normal deciduous forest fauna, the stag, the wild boar, the wolf, the brown bear, the otter, animals in fact with which we are familiar in Europe to-day. The urus was found also, and he only seems to have become extinct during the war, and may perhaps still survive. We may sum up the situation briefly by saying that the steppe fauna retreated entirely to the north and the forest fauna took its place.

We are now approaching modern times and a modern type of climate. The fauna of neolithic times is the direct descendant of the forest and meadow fauna which we have been discussing. One or two important changes took place. The lion became extinct, and two varieties of cattle, the short-horn (*Bos longifrons*) and the long-horn (*Bos taurus*), appeared. Our modern herds may probably claim them as their ancestors. Otherwise the fauna was very similar to that which we have already met. The eaters of flesh included the wolf, the fox, the cat, the marten, the otter, the badger, and the brown bear. The herbivorous animals were the bison, the red and fallow deer, the moose, the beaver, horses, rabbits, hares and squirrels. We find the ancestors of the modern domestic flocks and herds which either migrated or were introduced by man into Europe at this period.

Although the configuration of the outlying parts of Western Europe has changed considerably since neolithic times, and though we know that there have been and still are changes going on in the level of the snow-line of the Alps, there has been no very great general climatic change. The most fundamental difference between palæolithic times, taken as a whole, and Azilian-Neolithic-Modern times is the change we have already discussed from a continental to an oceanic type of climate and surroundings.

In Magdalenian times the northern shore of the Bay of Biscay probably stretched far to the westward, more than 10° west of Greenwich. Apart from a period of depression which may probably be correlated with Mousterian times,[1] we have evidence that the principal palæolithic stations were well inland. Great Britain was not an island; the warm currents from the Gulf of Mexico did not wash the shores which they do to-day.

The extent of these changes is easy to describe but

[1] It has unfortunately been necessary to allude to certain palæolithic periods in this chapter. A full discussion of their significance will, however, be found in that which follows.

difficult sometimes exactly to realize. Some excavations which were made in Malta some years ago bring
home perhaps more than anything else the profound
changes which have taken place. Malta is at present
a small island, round the whole of which it is possible
to go in one day. The space is extremely restricted,
and every available inch of land is cultivated. In
palæolithic times, however, this island seems to have
formed a buttress on the great land bridge from Europe
to Africa, and hippopotami wallowed in the pools of a
great lake which seems to have been fresh water.
To-day every drop of rain water is carefully conserved;
in palæolithic times there was sufficient water to cut
a valley, the Weid Dalam, which is about a hundred
feet across at the top, and the sides of the valley are
deeply undercut by the swirling of waters. Such
changes are so very visible that they are more impres-
sive perhaps to the eye even than the change which
has separated our own island from the mainland.

This very brief survey then may help us to realize,
at least to some extent, the raw materials which were
available for use by primitive man. The use that he
made of them will be discussed in the chapter which
follows.

PART III
TYPES AND STAGES OF LABOUR

CHAPTER VIII

THE EARLIEST ARTS OF HUMAN LIFE

Palæolithic Man

OUR inquiry has up to the present been of a general nature. We have studied the conditions which govern primitive labour from the point of view of man himself and also from the point of view of his environment. Such generalities have the disadvantage that they give but an inadequate picture of primitive man, because we must necessarily quest through the world for examples with which to illustrate our statements, and therefore our narrative must often fail because it becomes too abstract.

In the chapters which follow more detailed study will be made of certain peoples. The chapters have been arranged partly in chronological and partly in geographical order. In many cases it will be found that questions which were treated briefly in Part I are here worked out in greater detail. The student will also find in these chapters additional material which may be used to support, illustrate, and not infrequently to qualify, the statements which have been made earlier in the book.

It has been necessary in dealing with the earliest development of labour in prehistoric times to introduce a large amount of somewhat technical detail. This is inevitable if we are to understand the gradual evolution of man's arts which has taken place in Western Europe since it was first inhabited by man. The specialist may feel that in some cases we have generalized too much, but it must be remembered that our aim is not archæology but a right understanding of the problems which faced early man in his endeavour to wrest a living from the wilderness, armed as he was with instruments which seem to us very inadequate and of which we have probably only fragmentary remains.

The most primitive human implements known have formed the subject of considerable controversy, because it has often been difficult to decide whether they were human handiwork or whether the apparent flaking was not due entirely to natural causes. We know that nature can take chips off flint in one, possibly two ways; the first is usually described as thermal action. Changes in temperature, if they are rapid, cause uneven stresses in a material which make it split. Experimentally we can reproduce this action by pouring hot water into a cold glass or by turning up a lamp suddenly before the chimney has had time to warm.

We are not familiar with this type of natural thermal action in England, because the climatic changes are usually gradual. In tropical countries, however, especially in desert regions where there is little vegetation to check radiation, the stones and rocks become very hot during the day, but as soon as the sun sets there is a rapid cooling, and even large rocks will split. In earlier times, when, as we have shown, Europe had a warmer climate, stones may have split in this way.

Again, in a cold climate, water gets into the cracks of a stone and freezes. Ice occupies more space than water, and the cracks are enlarged, and eventually the stone splits. During colder periods this process may have been going on all over Western Europe. During times of warm summers and cold winters— a true northern continental climate—thermal action of both types may occur.

The second method whereby Nature flakes flints is by direct pressure; the edge of a flint is brought in the soil against some hard substance, another flint or a piece of hard rock, and a flake is pressed off.

Man fashions stone implements in ways which are not dissimilar from those of nature, but he has a further method, usually termed the percussion method, which can rarely occur in nature. It is always possible that thermal action may have been used in early times for making implements. We cannot be certain of this, for it is not possible to distinguish between flints split by fire intentionally and those split by nature.

We have, however, a record of the one people, the Andamanese, who appear before the arrival of the white man to have fashioned rude implements by putting stones into the fire. This is a natural and simple technique, easily discovered by any people in possession of fire, for the stones of an open hearth rapidly split.

The method of flaking by freezing does not appear to have been used by primitive man. Flaking by pressure is in its earliest forms easy, in its latest development, towards the end of the Stone Age, a very difficult accomplishment. If a thin piece of flint is held in the hand and pressure exerted, with a piece of wood or bone, across this edge, small flakes may be chipped off.

The method will be understood most easily by actually experimenting with a piece of road metal which has already been broken into thin flakes, and the handle of a tooth-brush. It will be found very easy to detach minute chips, but to make the edge follow any particular form or to take off larger chips needs greater practice and skill.

The third human method of working flints is to detach flakes by blows from a hammer-stone. It will be found that if a series of flakes are detached in this way there arises from the flake just distal to the place where the blow was struck a hemispherical protuberance known as the "bulb of percussion." On the summit of this a small scar will be seen. The bulb is so situated in relation to the surface which was struck that the plane of this surface from a chord to the circumference of the bulb is about a third of the distance from the circumference to the centre. Further down the flake will be found a series of concentric arcs, whose centre is the bulb of percussion. On the core from which the flake was struck off these features are reversed, there being a hollow corresponding to the bulb. Both the percussion and pressure methods are used to make an elaborate instrument.

The earliest work flints known are rough flint nodules from which flakes have been taken. Although in some cases efforts have been made apparently to shape the flint as a whole, man's ingenuity has rather been directed to retouching a natural stone to give it an edge and to suit it to the actual requirements than to shape the whole implement to a standard pattern. These early types have received various names. Perhaps the most satisfactory is pre-Chellean.

Some of the pre-Chellean represent quite elaborate and advanced forms, and there is little doubt that they have a long history behind them. At present, however, little definite is known of this history, and, although we may feel convinced that many of the earlier forms are genuine human tools, we can say little or nothing of the industries for which they were used.

About six types of pre-Chellean implements have been recognized. First, the " hammer-stone " with which all the rest were made, easily recognizable by its abraded edge where many blows have been given; " scrapers " are also recognizable. We know that modern primitive tribes use a stone-scraper for cleaning the fat off skins. A third type is known to French archæologists as the *grattoir*, which is often translated as " plane " or " planing tool." These implements have a steep-sided, rather rounded edge. The name " plane " is apt to be misleading, as it suggests to most of us an implement for smoothing a cut surface of wood or metal. The purpose of these tools was, however, much more likely to have been cleaning of hides or sinews. A fourth type appears to have been used as a drill or boring implement, a fifth as a primitive substitute for a knife.

We also find the prototypes of what developed in later times into the *coup de poing* or hand-axe, which we shall discuss later. All these implements are simply stones retouched to give them a convenient edge to make them fit for the hand. We do not know whether they were directly grasped or whether they were fastened in some form of grip; the analogy of modern peoples would suggest the latter method, but it is not safe to press the analogy too far.

In the succeeding or " Chellean " period—so-called from the type-station of "Chelles " on the Marne—a clearly recognizable type of implement is found, the so-called *coup de poing*. This implement is flat, almond-shaped, some of the crust being left at the blunt end. These implements may have been hafted, but many fit the hand so well that it is possible that they were used unmounted. They vary in length from four to about eight inches, though longer specimens have been found.

The *coup de poing*, of which the exact use has been lost and forgotten, appears to have played an important part in the history of human endeavour. A similar type of instrument has a very wide distribution, and though a closer inspection reveals local differences, the general type is the same. There is unfortunately no people that has preserved the use of such an instrument to the present date. The recently extinct Tasmanians had an analogue, but it differed in some ways from the familiar type. We have not among our metal tools anything to compare with it in form.

The arrow-head is similar in type all the world over; the tomahawk, the stone celt or axe, and the modern hatchet, present an unmistakable likeness. The general tendency of tools has been to specialize towards an edge or a point, and only a few modern implements possess both. For example, the knife that every Sudanese carries is triangular and can be used to pierce or cut; the tendency of our modern knives is to possess a blade for cutting and a spike for piercing. The *coup de poing* appears to stand at the very beginning of all heavy hand tools, and to be the forerunner of what has now developed into the axe, adze, mattock, heavy knife, and probably spear and sword.

Sollas has called attention to the fact that the Tasmanian aborigines used a similar implement for climbing trees; the *coup de poing* may have been used for this purpose, in forested districts, but we find similar weapons in Africa on sites which show little evidence of ever having been forested. We must therefore suppose that the implement was much more widely used. In addition to this general tool we find implements whose purpose appears to have been similar to those we have met with previously, hammer-stones, scrapers, borers, " planes."

The succeeding or " Acheulean " period, coincident with a drier climate, has a wider distribution; possibly some of the old forest marsh had been uninhabitable. The old sites continued to be inhabited, especially where, as in the valleys of the Somme, the Marne and the Seine, the flint is good. A Southern France quartzite was used, possibly owing to the absence of good flint. New and important sites began, such as Lavallois, near Paris, from which the " Lavallois " flakes are named, and Wolvercote, just north of the boundary of the City of Oxford. Another " type " station of Acheulean times is La Micoque, in the Vézère basin in South-Western France, where miniature flints were manufactured.

Apart from these special stations, however, a remarkably uniform type of culture appears to have been distributed over Western Europe in Acheulean times, except in Scandinavia and in the neighbourhood of the Alps, where the great extension of glaciers probably made life impossible. It has been suggested that this wide distribution of culture was due to the migratory habits of the people, but the period was an immensely long one, and it is not impossible that in such a time a uniform culture may have spread, especially if geographical conditions were comparatively similar.

The Acheulean *coup de poing* is more developed than the Chellean. At the beginning there are two main types, the so-called " lance-pointed "—or as the French archæologists call them, the barge-pole type (*ficron*), a simple flaked broad point with a large base and a

pointed oval type. The latter differ from the Chellean
in being slightly smaller, beautifully symmetrical and
flaked all over the surface. They have been subdivided into four types, almond, oval-almond,
elongated oval and sub-triangular.

Their use has been widely disputed. Commont
believes that they were not weapons of war, and that
they were gripped in the hand, even in those cases
where, unlike the older Chellean weapons, they have not
the convenient blunt grip. Obermaier, on the other
hand, has suggested that they were fixed in a shaft,
and that they were either weapons of war or of the
chase. There is also a third type of *coup de poing* with
a chisel edge, forming a primitive type of axe. Some
authors would see at this period a definite specialization
into " industrial " and " fighting " weapons, for in
addition to the new types mentioned above, the old
scrapers and borers continue with a further addition
of a " point," which may well have been a spear-head.
At this time use began to be made of flakes as well as
flint nodules for implements, and towards the end of
Acheulean times there was a general development of
the type.

Contemporary with this evolution of culture we find,
as we have already shown, a change in climate from
a warm temperate to a dry almost continental type.
Later Acheulean implements have been found actually
imbedded in " loess "—a dusty layer of soil only found
under the dry, windy condition of open steppe. There
is no essential change in the type of implement used.
The technique is better, the form is the same.

The contrast with the Chellean forms is striking,
but the same general principles are at work, and we
can trace a gradual evolution with no great mutations
all through these two periods. All that remain are

stone implements; wood naturally would be hardly likely to have survived. If bone implements of any number had been used, we should have expected to have found them, for in succeeding periods they are numerous enough. We have, as yet, however, no traces of any bone implements whatever.

Acheulean, Chellean and pre-Chellean men were probably hunters, for we know that the earliest stage in human development was the hunting stage. We do not know exactly how they caught their game, for the stone implements which have been described are all that have survived. We do know, however, that they lived in a deciduous forest, except in late Acheulean times; such forests provide a good deal of vegetable food, some of which—blackberries, for instance—we still eat. We know from the remains of some blackberry seeds inside a neolithic woman's skeleton that they were eaten plentifully by the people of the new Stone Age. Probably they were relished by the older man. Wild crab-apples, hips and haws and mountain ash berries are all edible and plentiful in this type of forest. Animals of the bigger and smaller varieties were plentiful and were eaten by man, and the bigger bones split for the sake of the marrow they contained.

If we can rely on the analogies of modern hunting tribes we should suppose that the people were very nomadic, wandering, as the eaters of flesh always do, in search of game. But we find in both Chellean and Acheulean times that certain stations were frequented over long periods, whether continuously or not we do not know. Why did the hunter, if hunter he was, come back to the same place, century after century? Geography probably gives us the clue to the difficulty. First, he needed flint to make his implements, and, as the population in industrial times has followed coal and iron, so in primitive times it followed flint.

A second reason, also, may have had an important influence. A damp wood is an unpleasant place to live in; the boar and the bull may wallow in the mud of a forest swamp, the elephant may crash through the undergrowth, but these animals have a hide which protects them. We do not know what covering early man had, but there is no reason to believe that it was sufficient for him to live at his ease in a primeval temperate forest.

There were open spaces, either high open downs or heaths, or the edges of rivers, where the forest did not dominate, and it was no doubt in such places that he would have found it easiest to live. Now it is precisely in the river-gravels that we do find the clearest and most frequent examples of the earliest man. The form of his habitation we do not know. Some of the anthropoid apes make shelters of boughs, so we may suppose that he has some form of shelter near his flint workshop and near his fire.

Of his clothing we know nothing. The continual presence of scrapers even from early times suggests that hides were prepared and used. The Australian aborigines, who do not wear any clothing, however, use scrapers, but they live in a warm climate, whereas Western Europe, even in the genial interglacial periods, can never have been very warm in winter. Skins of some sort may well have been used. We can say nothing of trade or transport, but the fact that flints travelled sometimes in a " raw " state over considerable distances suggests that some form of trade may have taken place, as the distribution is too great to be explained solely by the theory of migrations.

Archæologists have, as we have shown, divided up

Acheulean implements, and even those of earlier date, into weapons of war and the chase, on the one hand, and industrial implements on the other. The analogy of modern tribes would suggest that the hunting and probably the skinning of the larger animals was in the hands of the men; skinning of small animals and home industries the work of the women. A man also makes his own tools.

It has been shown that among modern hunting peoples seeds and berries are collected by the women in autumn; we may suppose that such collecting formed part of the duties of palæolithic women. This brief sketch of the types of labour which fell to the lot of these early men is necessarily incomplete, because we have so little evidence. We do not know how far one tribe differed from another. The evidence suggests that there was in Western Europe a fairly uniform culture; there are, however, certain sites, Lavallois, for instance, where the technique appears to be better than elsewhere, suggesting either a local school of more brilliant craftsmen or else a more advanced state of life in which the struggle for existence was less hard and the workers had more time to acquire a specialized skill.

The Acheulean period was succeeded by one which has received the name of Mousterian. Physically, the Mousterians belonged to the type which inhabited Europe during the earlier periods but which became extinct after Mousterian times. Some archæologists have been inclined on the grounds of the type of artefacts belonging to this period to group Mousterian man rather with those who come after than with those who came before him. It seems clear, however, that such a position is untenable. Mousterian forms are foreshadowed in the flake industry which accompanied

Acheulean and, it may be added, even the early Chellean *coup de poing*. On the other hand the old Mousterian *coup de poing* develops directly from that of the late Acheulean period. In many instances it is nearly, if not quite, as well made.

The type station from which this period receives its name is Le Moustier, on the Vézère, in the Dordogne district of South-Western France, the home of palæolithic man probably for many thousands of years. Finds have, however, been made as far west as Devonshire and Northern Spain, and as far east as the great bend of the Danube. Remains of this period have been found on the open sites of the old Acheulean people in the valleys of the Thames, the Somme and the Marne. Nearly a hundred years ago Kent's hole in Devonshire was explored, and we now know that this was a Mousterian site. Dr. Marett has found in a cave in Jersey numerous implements and flakes.

The Dordogne region, in addition to the type station already mentioned, is especially rich in sites. In Spain at least two sites have been reported on the north coast and one near the headwaters of the Tagus. There is a famous site at Spy on the Meuse, famous because of the actual human remains found there, and four on the Rhine. Of these there is one near the source of the river, the cave of Wildkirchli, high up in the Alps, and known in romance and legend long before archæologists discovered that its first inhabitants were Mousterian.[1]

Six, possibly seven, sites are known in Germany,

[1] Readers of Ekkehard, written by von Scheffel, and the German equivalent of Charles Reade's "Cloister and the Hearth," will remember that the writing of one of the early German epics is placed by the author, quite unhistorically, in this cave in the high Alps, near the source of the Rhine and Rhone.

and others in Austria and Hungary. Some of these sites in Central Europe are of special interest, because they are actually within or close to the icefields. Wildkirchli, for instance, is 5,000 feet high, and is even now close to the limit of perpetual snow. Sirgenstein, on the upper waters of the Danube, is also a site of interest and importance, because it contains complete stratification of archæological material from Mousterian to neolithic times.

Mousterian implements have been subdivided by archæologists into smaller periods. The differences, however, throw little light and hardly represent changed types of craftsmanship so much as a gradual evolution of the same type. It is sometimes stated that the fundamental tool of earlier times, the *coup de poing*, has almost disappeared, and that when it is found it represents merely a degenerate form. These implements are, however, quite abundant in the Mousterian of the Somme, at Le Moustier itself in the lowest and the highest floors, but not in the strata in between, at Combe-Capelle and elsewhere.

The typical Mousterian implements are, however, not made from the core or flint nodule as had been done in previous periods, but from the flakes which were struck off and worked to the form which was required. The Mousterian " point " would be chosen, perhaps, as representing the best Mousterian industry. But, though the implements show greater variety, they do not present any forms which can be definitely associated with a purpose unassociated with the earlier implements. The technique is less skilful, and some archæologists see in this period not so much the feeble beginnings of a new age as the last remains of the great *coup de poing* industry which had flourished for so long. But we find that bone implements are beginning to be used, and, as we shall see later, bone played an important part in succeeding cultures.

It is possible to take modern analogies that the use of bone implements may be associated with a cold climate. We find a number of bone implements, for instance, at Wildkirchli, which, as we have shown, was actually within the ice-sheet. Stone cannot be excavated from a frozen subsoil, and the dwellers in a cold climate must needs eat large quantities of flesh if they are to keep warm. We may therefore associate this beginning of bone culture with a cold climate. We have shown, then, that physically Mousterian man belongs to the old; culturally he belongs for the most part to the new. We may therefore either classify him with the new or, as some do, as a transitional stage.

The growing rigours of climate had an important effect on one side of the arts of life, namely, the choice of habitation. We have seen how in earlier days most of the sites were placed in what may have been open spaces in the forest. Mousterian men did not abandon these old sites, but they began to inhabit caves. The legend of the mediaeval hermit of Wildkirchli sharing his cave with a bear may have been fanciful, but there seems every reason to suppose that Mousterian man did. We can hardly agree with the pleasant but fanciful picture of a recent writer, who suggests that in Mousterian times we have for the first time in human history the faint realization of a home with the children playing round the fire, the women cooking and preparing skins. The continued occupation of earlier sites suggests that man had already his favourite places of abode.

In Mousterian times, on the other hand, it may be suggested that the camping-place varied with the seasons; in the winter, or possibly in summer, if he went on the ice he used the shelter of a cave; in summer he followed the migrations of animals as the Eskimo does to-day, and had his summer dwelling. His " points " suggest more definitely than earlier weapons the use of spear or dart, and discoidal stones may, as some suggest, have been used for throwing or as scrapers. Apart from cave life, however, we have little to add to what has already been said of the arts of life of these early folk.

The succeeding Aurignacian period corresponds, as we have shown, with the retreat of the glaciers. The people whose skeletons we now find in Europe are not unlike ourselves. Their industry has developed far from that of the Mousterians. The distribution of Aurignacian stations is not dissimilar from that of the Mousterian, in fact in many cases the same places certainly contain both Aurignacian and Mousterian implements, but the sites in Germany are more numerous, and an Aurignacian cave has been found in England as far north as Langwith Bassett in Derby-shire. This greater extension of sites is probably due to the presence of a more genial climate and the retreat of the ice-sheet, rendering a wider extension possible.

The implements are generally similar to the Mousterian in technique, that is to say they are made of flakes which have been struck off and dressed on one side only. The forms, however, are different, showing both an evolutionary change, that is to say a direct development from forms with which we are already familiar, and also a new series which had not previously been observed. Most striking of all is the absence of the *coup de poing*, so characteristic of the earliest periods, but already decadent and on the verge of extinction in Mousterian times.

In addition to the hunting and industrial weapons
we have also met, there begins in Aurignacian times
a series of tools which seem to be associated with art.
The whole period may be conveniently divided into
three parts, and the variety of the implements suggests
that at this time labour was highly developed and
specialized, even though each man may have used
many tools. The lower Aurignacian is characterized
by the Chatelperron points, " angle-gravers," which
recall a modern graving instrument except for the fact
that they have straight not rounded edges, end-
scrapers and, in bone, the beginnings of what are
known as split-base points.

In the middle period the typical implements are
keeled scrapers and long flakes which are retouched
all round, beaked gravers and blades that are usually
called " strangled " owing to their being thinner in
the middle. The bone implements are of three types.
First, there are points with a split base, then leaf-
shaped points which are not split, and finally
cylindrical points, which are pointed at both ends.

The typical implements of the upper Aurignacian
are first the " La Gravette points." These implements
were probably used as knives, not as etching tools.
End-scrapers not retouched all round were used, and
simple gravers. The second part of this period is
characterized by what are known as " Font Robert "
points, which are shaped not unlike a simple arrow-
head, with a tang but no barbs. They are often
retouched at the point on the reverse side. Shouldered
points are also found, and are probably derived from
the La Gravette type. The outline of this form is
not unlike the outline of a pointed carving-knife when
cast in one piece, although not, of course, so big. One
side is straight from base to tip, the other has a

projection or shoulder about the end of the lower third of its length. The purpose of this shoulder is probably hafting. The bone implements are points cut obliquely at the base.

We are now in a position to consider the life and industry of the Aurignacian people as a whole. The main method of obtaining food seems to have been by hunting. Aurignacian art shows an acquaintance with certain animals, so intimate and so vivid that it can hardly have been gained without close study. The animals represented include the mammoth, the woolly rhinoceros, the reindeer, the cave bear, wild cattle, the horse and the ibex. With the exception of the rhinoceros and the bear, all these animals belong to genera which have been intimately associated with man.

The wilder tribes to-day in Africa eat elephant with relish when such flesh is available; Aurignacian man may well have enjoyed rhinoceros; at least we find great quantities of his bones in Aurignacian caves. Bear steaks were a favourite dish even in Europe when the brown bear was commoner. Horses appear from the number of bones found to have formed a favourite diet. The number of bones of all these animals and the accuracy with which they are drawn suggests skilful hunting, and better methods than the hand to hand blow.

We have evidence which may be interpreted as showing that shafted weapons were used in the so-called *bâtons de commandement*. These are pieces of the antlers of reindeer with a straight round hole drilled through them. It has been suggested that these may be arrow straighteners. Similar implements of horn and bone are used by the Eskimo, with the important exception that the hole is always bored *obliquely*, not straight, as in most palæolithic specimens. Some of the small pointed flakes may have been used for " gorges," either for catching fish or animals. A gorge is wrapped in a piece of fish or meat, and, when swallowed, sticks in the gullet. The numerous Aurignacian hearths show that man was now well acquainted with fire, but no vessels have been found which could be used for boiling meat.

Both open sites and caves were used as habitations, and the great deposits of bones and flint flakes suggest that they were often used over long periods. The abundance of " scrapers " indicates that frequent use was made of hides, whether for clothing or for any other purpose it is impossible to say.

It is not within the scope of this work to discuss " æsthetic arts," but we cannot pass over the beautiful artistic work of Aurignacian man without a mention. Such of their art as has survived consists of representations of the human figure and animals, sculptured in high and low relief, etched on bone, and painted with ochre; all the work was done in outline, shading being unknown. The success and accuracy of this work, which contrasts in its simplicity of outline and clearness of form with the barbaric crudeness of much savage art, is strong evidence to support the view that man was sufficiently advanced in the arts which administer to the bare necessities of life to have a little leisure.

The Solutrean period, which next claims our attention, presents many features which are unusual, and the exact position of the culture is not clear. Before discussing the evidence in detail it may be stated in general terms that though the Solutrean certainly follows the Aurignacian and precedes the Magdalenian, it does not appear to divide them culturally.   Further, we find that in some respects the Magdalenian follows the Aurignacian, and some phases of neolithic work follow the Solutrean.

The distribution is also puzzling. Aurignacian culture is widely spread in Western and even in Central Europe. Solutrean, on the other hand, is comparatively local, and there is at present no evidence that it occurs in the Mediterranean area. On the other hand, it is not impossible that the Solutrean industry may have had a more northerly extension, possibly even into the Scandinavian Peninsula, than has hitherto been supposed.

If we consider the evidence in greater detail the following points of importance emerge. At the shelter of La Colombière, where up to the present no evidence of a Solutrean industry has been discovered, there is a floor which is placed stratigraphically in between the upper Aurignacian and the Magdalenian. It contains an "atypical" upper palæolithic industry and numerous drawings on stones and fragments of bone which are too developed for Aurignacian, but at the same time are not Magdalenian either in technique or spirit. The discoverers, Mayet and Pissot, describe this floor as upper Aurignacian; Breuil however suggests, quite tentatively, that this is a station where we "catch," almost as it were in an instantaneous photograph, the transition directly from Aurignacian to Magdalenian.

That such a difficulty should occur may at first sight seem strange. It is true that there are certain typical Solutrean implements, namely, laurel-leaf and shouldered points and a few borers and scrapers. In any ordinary Solutrean station, however, apart from these implements, the greater part of the industry is indistinguishable from an upper Aurignacian or lower

Magdalenian. In Hungary, on the other hand, the laurel-leaf points are found unaccompanied by any such industry. From this it seems reasonable to infer that the peculiar characters of the Solutrean industry in Western Europe are due to culture-contact, in other words, that the industries of the west were merely affected but not changed by the influence of a more eastern culture.

The origin of this culture and the causes of its disappearance are, however, still to seek. Further than this there appear to have been varying degrees of culture contact at different times during the Solutrean period. The upper Solutrean, characterized by shouldered points, is more local than the middle, which is associated with the laurel-leaf points. It is confined to France, where it occurs only between the Loire and the Pyrenees. The suggestion has been made that it represents the application of Solutrean technique to upper Aurignacian forms.

The evidence further suggests what may be described as Aurignacio-Magdalenian influences round the borders of the upper Solutrean district, a condition which has not been proved to exist, although its existence can hardly be doubted. As a definite example we may quote the wall engraving of a bison found in a cave at La Grèze in the Dordogne. The engraving is in the Aurignacian traditional style, although better executed, but is almost certainly Solutrean.

The bone industry tells a tale similar to that which is told by the flint. At some stations, Jean-Blancs for instance, it is almost indistinguishable from lower Magdalenian. Summing up, then, we may say that there is a great deal of evidence to suggest that there is no real break in the continuity, and that the traditions and influences which may be described as Aurignacio-Magdalenian were active all through the Solutrean period.

It has been said—unkindly, it would appear—that Solutrean man was deficient in artistic sense. It is true that he does not show evidence of possessing the æsthetic tradition of Aurignacian man, and some of the representations of mammoths which have been credited to him are probably Magdalenian in date, but the flint-work of Solutrean times is only, if ever, excelled by the finest examples of neolithic work. The Solutrean points are long and thin with ripple flaking, and it is extraordinarily difficult to copy them. The use of " pressure " flaking, which we have already described, was probably due to Solutrean initiative. Some of the finest and thinnest of these " laurel-leaf " points can hardly have had any practical value, as they are too thin and fragile to be used as spear-heads. In addition to these ceremonial spear-heads, however, we find smaller and more practical ones, " shouldered " points, which were no doubt hafted, borers, drills, awls, etching points and a number of bone implements.

The closing period of palæolithic culture, called Magdalenian from the type-station of La Madaleine (Dordogne) was, as we have shown, not a direct continuation or evolution from Solutrean culture, but rather a development of Aurignacian culture. The distribution of Magdalenian culture is of wide extent, and not localized as the Solutrean appears to be, although there are localities where we might have expected to find traces of Magdalenian man, but where as yet no definite evidence has been discovered. Undoubted stations of Magdalenian date occur in France, Belgium, England, Germany and Austria, especially in the area between the Rhine and Danube, and even far away to the east on the borders of Russia. In Spain stations have been found on the north coast, but as yet the Mediterranean area has failed to yield definite traces. In this area we find Azilian culture directly on top of Aurignacian.

It is in many ways natural that Magdalenian culture should have the type of distribution which our present knowledge indicates, for as we shall show it is essentially a culture bound up with a nomadic life in a cold climate, and even when Northern Europe was Arctic tundra, to take the extreme, the Mediterranean can hardly have been more than cold temperate, and may have had hot summers even if the winters were severe; a type of climate quite unsuited to the reindeer nomad which Magdalenian man seems to have been.

The flint industry with its fine and artistic technique became unimportant as compared with bone and horn. To a certain extent we may seek a cause in changing climates, for under cold conditions it is extremely difficult to get good workable flints. Those near the surface become fractured by the frosts, and those lying beyond the range of the frost cannot be reached. For many of the requirements of a race living under cold conditions, bone is much more suitable, and we find among the modern Eskimo that, although both bone and stone implements were used, the former predominated, and, except for scrapers, where a sharpened flint makes an ideal instrument, were much more suited to the conditions of life.

Magdalenian culture has been divided roughly into three divisions, although Breuil has a more elaborate division into six sub-periods. In the earliest period the climate seems to have corresponded to tundra; the middle may be described as a transitional stage, and in the upper Magdalenian the moist tundra had definitely changed into a cold dry steppe climate.

The industries of this period are usually distinguished by the bone rather than by the flint implements, as the latter carry on the traditions of earlier times, although flint drills are particularly numerous. Lower Magdalenian may be distinguished by bone points, which are flattened at the base. Secondly, short points are found which are cut obliquely and grooved, it has been suggested for poison. The art of the period may be briefly summarized; it includes the conventionalized drawings on bone which have been found at Placard, geometrical designs found at Marsoulas and Cap Blanc, to mention two stations only, and early sculptures which have also been found at Cap Blanc and at Lussac.

The middle period is the age of the finest sculptures, the *contours decoupés*, and the bas-reliefs. Primitive harpoons are also found at this level. In the third (upper) period the characteristic implement is the harpoon. During the earlier part of the sub-period they have only one row of barbs. This type of harpoon coincides with the finest drawings. In the later period the harpoons have two barbs, and there is a marked degeneration of the drawing and the bas-relief. In very late Magdalenian times borers with a curved point are also found. They have been called from a fanciful resemblance to a parrot's beak, *bec de perroquet*.

These details will serve to indicate the great differences which existed even during a single period in palæolithic times. If we sum up the evidence the types of labour which fell to Magdalenian man may be described as follows : The nature of the food quest had altered, or at least had considerably developed since earlier times, and was probably more successfully carried out. Man was armed with two weapons which make for greater efficiency in hunting and fishing, a barbed harpoon and a spear-thrower, although the absolute truth of this statement can never be proved, because it is always possible that at some previous date these implements may have been made of wood, as they are among modern savages to-day. It has been suggested with every appearance of probability that the harpoons were used to point fish spears such as used by some of the North American Indian tribes to-day.

The representation of barbed weapons in conjunction with animals of the chase also suggests that they were used for hunting as well as for fishing. The spear-thrower would aid considerably in projecting them. A weapon of this type is used by many peoples to-day, especially the Eskimo and certain American tribes and the Australians. It consists essentially of a small piece of wood or bone, with a raised nick at the end. The butt-end of the shaft of the spear is fitted along the spear-thrower, which is grasped in the fingers of the right hand. The butt of the spear fits in the nick at the end. The spear-thrower adds length to the arm, and enables a spear to be thrown both a greater distance and with greater accuracy.

The continual occurrence of reindeer both in pictorial and sculptural representation, and also in the remains of " food dumps " and among the collection of weapons and rubbish on a site, has given rise to the suggestion that certainly at this time, if not earlier, man had begun to have that close relationship with that animal which some modern tundra tribes have. As we shall show, however, in a later chapter, there is considerable evidence which suggests that on the contrary reindeer nomadism is of comparatively recent origin; but it is certain that man was very familiar with the herds and depended on them for many of the essential weapons and tools which made life possible.

Magdalenian man lived in caves, but his remains have been found in open stations, and it is not impossible, especially if he followed the migrating herds of reindeer, that he had summer as well as winter houses. The number of needles and fine " points," which probably served as drills for the eyes of needles, suggests an elaborate " sewing " technique adapted certainly to the making of clothing, and also possibly to the manufacture of tents or some migratory form of dwelling.

The number of scrapers and similar implements suggests that skins were used in large quantities, no doubt for some domestic purpose. The use of skins by the Eskimo for boats and canoes lends credence to the theory that possibly Magdalenian man may have used this convenient form of transport especially for fishing. We have evidence which suggests but does not at present confirm the theory that man has now reached a stage which is passing beyond that of the primitive hunter.

There can be little doubt that considerable specialization had taken place in the forms of implements and in the material used. Stone is no longer used as a general and only material for all purposes. On the contrary it has ceased to be the principal material. Bone, ivory and horn take the most prominent place. Wood may have been used, but it would not, of course, have survived; but we do find such a complete armoury of weapons and tools among the things that have survived that it is not unreasonable to suppose that it was not much used; it is also possible that the

climatic conditions of Western Europe at the time may
not have favoured the growth of sufficient forest to
provide the necessary material, a reason that certainly
encourages some modern tribes to use bone and horn
weapons. We have, however, shown that there is
reason to believe that the forest trees of Europe were
not dissimilar from what they are to-day. It is
difficult, on the other hand, to estimate how much
timber was available for man; probably a good
deal.

We have therefore no adequate solution for the
difficulty why bone and horn should be used, except
that savage man probably found that the soft-wooded
forest trees were unsuitable for many purposes, and
bone being a general material was used more widely
than was quite necessary. The art of Magdalenian
times is one of the wonders which have been recently
revealed to us, especially by the French School of
Archæology. Its accuracy of feeling and beauty of
colour suggest a freshness and a mastery of technique
which has only to be seen to be admired. But as
æsthetic art does not contribute to the necessities of
life we must regretfully pass it by.

The close of the palæolithic period, or perhaps what
may be better called an intermediate period between
the old and the new Stone Age, is known by the title
of the Azilian and Tardenoisian periods. Some
authors would join these two and refer to the period
as the Azilian-Tardenoisian. The two type stations
are the Mas d'Azil in the Pyrenees and Fère à
Tardenois in Northern France. The majority of
stations occur in the Pyrenees, but a small group are
found in the Dordogne, and isolated sites are scattered
over Western Europe.

The typical Azilian implement is a small flat

harpoon made out of red-deer horn ; borers and scrapers occur, but they do not show the variety or skilled technique of Magdalenian times, and there seems to be a tendency to return to the *grattoir caréné* of Aurignacian times. Tardenoisian culture is character- ized by a number of pygmy flints—or microliths. The exact purpose of these flints is not fully under- stood. A comparison with a similar culture in Africa has suggested that man for some time was largely snail-eating, and that these stones were used for remov- ing the animals from their shells.

We have now followed the progress of certain branches of palæolithic culture from its earliest dim beginnings to its final culmination in the Solutrean and Magdalenian periods. Let us review briefly what progress man made during that immensely long period of time, and how far he moved from living to " living well."

The earliest remains show only a few flints which have been retouched, but whose essential natural form has not been altered. A gradual mastery over flint technique was acquired, and later to a large extent abandoned in favour of weapons and tools of bone and horn. The weapon held in the hand was replaced by a hafted weapon, and in Magdalenian times there is definite and clear evidence of an implement for adding to the throwing capacity of the arm.

Throughout this long period there is a tendency to specialize tools. The earlier *coup de poing* was probably used for many purposes. In Magdalenian times the number and variety of implements suggest that each was used for a single definite purpose. Throughout the whole period man appears to have been a hunter, but the presence of the harpoon in Magdalenian times suggests he also became a fisherman. We have no evidence that he supplemented his diet with domestic plants or animals.

In the earlier periods, man appears to have lived in open stations; during the second part of the palæolithic age he utilized caves for at least part of the year. We have no evidence of the type of clothing that he used, but the Magdalenian needles suggest that he had mastered the art of sewing. The numerous scrapers of a much earlier period suggest the use of skins, and thorns may have been used to sew before bone. Towards the end of the palæolithic period labour had developed to a pitch which was sufficiently high to admit of æsthetic arts which show a mastery of technique unusual among any savage peoples.

Limited as we are by our ignorance of all types of labour in palæolithic times, except the arts of flint and bone working and of cave paintings and engravings on bone, it is impossible to paint a full picture of the conditions which prevailed. In most cases it would seem that they were far behind all modern savages, the greatest gaps in their knowledge being their ignorance of pottery and of domestic animals. There are, however, some modern savages who are ignorant of these most important elements in any culture.

CHAPTER IX

THE DEVELOPMENT OF LABOUR IN WESTERN EUROPE

Neolithic Man

IN describing the conditions of labour among the palæolithic peoples we are dealing for the most part with a stage of culture which is not generally very familiar and whose traces, though they are widely spread, need considerable skill to identify and to classify. With neolithic man it is otherwise. In many parts of England the ploughman continually turns up implements, especially arrow-heads, and certainly in some parts of Oxfordshire many of the National schools have a small typical collection of these implements. The presence of so many neolithic implements suggests that neolithic man was widely scattered over Western Europe, and that no great change has taken place to cover up the remains of his industry. A careful study of the remains, however, suggests that the whole country was not inhabited but only those parts which from their upland situation or exposed position were not covered with thicket or forest.

We are fortunate in our knowledge of the neolithic arts of life. In Northern Europe he has left behind him great shell heaps, the remains of his kitchen refuse, which give us a clear idea of the animals with which he was familiar. In the Alps, possibly, it is

true, at a somewhat later period, he lived in pile dwellings or palafittes on the lakes. This circumstance,
owing to the preservative character of lake water and
bog moss, has preserved for our use not only stone
implements but even the very garments that he wore
and the corn that he grew. The picture therefore is
much more complete than could be expected or hoped
for.

The palafitte-dwelling man had advanced to a stage
of culture that was very high in comparison with that
of palæolithic man. At present we have no clear
evidence of the transition. We know, however, that
neolithic man was both a keeper of domestic animals
and an agriculturalist.

Dechelette has laid down clearly the method whereby
the archæologist may recognize whether animals were
domesticated or wild from the remains which are
found. He suggests four criteria. First, the
presence of complete skeletons implies that animals
were kept in captivity. If animals are merely hunted
the hunter brings back the skins and the joints, but
avoids carrying such parts of the carcass as are of no
value to him. Secondly, domestic animals are not
kept till they reach an extreme age, and therefore no
skeletons of aged individuals are found, whereas the
hunter takes any game that he can find, and often
aged individuals predominate because they are more
easily obtained. Thirdly, the hunters, generally
speaking, obtain an equal number of each sex, whereas
we know that in our herds the females predominate
because the young males are killed off early except for
a few individuals who are wanted for stud purposes.
The fourth criterion used by Dechelette is the resemblance to modern domestic species.

On this evidence it has been established that in the

palafittes the following domestic animals occurred—
the dog, the pig, the goat, the sheep, the ox and the
horse, although very few of the last named are found
till the Bronze Age. The ox together with the wild
deer are the commonest, in fact there are more bones
of these two animals than of all the rest put together.
It follows then that the commonest game animal was
the deer, which no doubt replaced the reindeer which
had played such an important part in the earlier stages
of culture. Steenstrup recognized the presence. of the
dog in the kitchen middens from the marks of his
teeth on the bones thrown out as kitchen refuse.

The dog seems to have been the only domestic
animal in the kitchen middens, and the long list of
animals we have given above by no means appear
together. Rather there is a succession of waves of
new domestic animals coming in. The pig and the
sheep, for instance, only appear slowly, and the late
appearance of the horse is of special interest, because
the species is the same as in palæolithic times.

It must not be supposed that everywhere the culture
was similar. At Anau, for instance, a site near
Askabad in Turkestan which was so carefully
excavated by Pumpelly,[1] the history of domestic
animals appears to have been somewhat different.
Here domestic animals are not found till ten feet of
debris had accumulated, when there are remains of the
Asiatic variety of the Urus. This is followed by the
pig. The true domestic sheep does not appear for a
long time, but it is preceded by varieties of a horned
mountain sheep. The camel appears about the same
time as the sheep and long before the horse, which
even on the steppes is a late comer as he is in Central

[1] Pumpelly, "Explorations in Turkestan," Carnegie
Institute Publications, Washington, No, 73, 1904, 2 Vols.

Europe. Here in Anau Pumpelly is inclined to believe that the agricultural life preceded the pastoral.

The palafittes have preserved for us a fairly complete account of neolithic agriculture. A very large number of species of plants are found. We know that they used three varieties of wheat, two of barley, and two of millet, including the Egyptian wheat and the six-rowed barley which is also an Egyptian species. The importance of the presence of these varieties will be realized from what has been said earlier in regard to the origin of agriculture. We find also the remains of those fruits which we are accustomed to associate with the forest and meadow-land we know so well in Europe to-day—nuts, plums, strawberries, apples and pears.

It is probable that neolithic man knew of the use of the grape, and before the coming of the Bronze Age of rye and oats. Poppy and caraway seeds were used to flavour their hard unleavened cakes, the flour for which was ground in a flat quern not unlike that which I have already referred to as being in use in Mexico to-day. I think it not improbable that the grain was first pounded in a wooden mortar, to judge from the practice of many primitive peoples to-day, but I have not been able to discover any record of one having been preserved.

These details all suggest that a comparatively elaborate stage of culture had been reached. The neolithic age is therefore particularly puzzling because of its local variations and because, though we are inclined to build up an elaborate picture and say that neolithic man was both agriculturalist and keeper of animals, it is extremely probable that both these occupations in many places were either carried on by different sexes or by different tribes.

The weapons and implements that he used were naturally somewhat elaborate. Bone was still used for pointed implements as it had been used in the previous period. Stone, however, was probably the most important material. I have used the word " probably " because it is impossible to judge the exact function that wood played in his life, and to judge by the analogy of modern savages this was not unlikely to have been great. Neolithic implements have been described as differing from palæolithic implements in being polished, a statement that needs qualification, because so long as stone implements were used many remained unpolished.

It has been suggested that the polishing of implements began almost accidentally. If any implement is used to dig in the soil the wearing part of it becomes polished by contact with the fine bits of sand and minerals in the soil. It would be a natural step to polish the whole implement and not merely the cutting edge, a process which can be done by rubbing it all over with sand. At the beginning of neolithic times, in what is known as the Campignian period, polishing does not seem to have been known, but we can trace in their implements the prototypes of the later polished axes or celts. Many of their implements are of the type which we have grown familiar with in studying older man, but they manufactured also long instruments which are usually known as " picks " and broad bladed axes. They also used horn and bone, and seem to have hunters and fishermen who, it has been suggested, followed the reindeer.

The full neolithic industry followed the development suggested by this early industry, and added or developed what may be described as saws, knives and spear-heads. The neolithic celt, seen in its earliest form in the Campignian industry, possesses all the essentials of a modern axe but one. It has the necessary weight; it has a cutting edge that is not too steep or brittle; it can be ground and sharpened when the cutting edge has gone. Mechanically, however, it is unsound.

In earlier neolithic times the only means of hafting it was to bind it to a piece of wood from which a bough had grown. The bough was lopped short and the main stock cut off just above the joint and at a convenient distance lower down. The implement was then fastened by sinew to the lower edge of the projecting bough. Thus it became an adze or mattock. The carpenter in Peking to-day fastens his adze to the haft by a not dissimilar method.

There was a second and even more unsatisfactory way of hafting the axe. It could be inserted in a cleft stick and bound firmly in place. This procedure is very unsatisfactory because every blow tends to loosen the hafting. This latter method has survived among some of the Pacific peoples to-day.

It was long before neolithic man discovered how to make a hole in his stone axe to receive the shaft. The earliest pierced axes have the hole ground from either side, probably with a stick twirled between the fingers and sand. A cup-shaped hollow was thus produced on either side, and the two met in the middle so that a stick could be driven through. But such a hole is inconvenient, as the haft cannot be firmly fixed, and man later discovered a way of drilling out a neat hole, probably by twirling a hollow stick or reed with sand from one side only. A cylindrical core would thus be cut out. The development was, however, a long one, and the flat celt survived long enough to be copied in bronze when the use of that metal became known.

Side by side with the development of polishing man learned, especially in Scandinavia and in Egypt, a wonderful technique in " pressure flaking," and made knives with a sharp edge and a blunt handle not unlike our modern knives in shape. He also hafted small flakes skilfully; he inserted them, for instance, in the jaw-bone of an animal, substituting flakes for teeth, a type of sickle which in shape at least has survived till modern times. He invented the arrow-head of the pattern which in its main form was never superseded in Western Europe. The earliest form was that of a leaf, which gradually developed two barbs, a familiar shape of which specimens can often be picked up on our ploughland.

Neolithic man also invented the use of pottery. There is beginning to be evidence of pottery in earlier times, but with the neolithic period its use becomes abundant and diverse. This pottery is usually classified into three groups—corded, banded, and caliciform. The first two classes depend on the ornament, and therefore are outside our present terms of reference. In Britain, at least, there seems to have been two different types of vessels, one a form with a narrow neck round which a sinew or withe was probably tied so that it could be lifted off the fire, and the second type with a long neck which tapers slightly outwards. How these pots were used we cannot of course know exactly.

Neolithic man's architecture is remarkable. He built the greater number of the rude stone monuments which form such a remarkable feature of the remains of prehistoric man in Western Europe and elsewhere. Their purpose seems for the most part to have been either religious or in memory of the dead. They do not seem to have played a part in the arts of life nor to have been concerned with the gaining of daily bread, and therefore are outside our present purpose. His domestic architecture was, however, none the less remarkable.

Three types of dwellings may be described. The first are simple hearths. It is not improbable that these hearths represent all that remains or has been discovered of larger villages or hamlets. These latter belong to the second class, the third being usually classed from the abundant remains of industry that have been discovered as ateliers or workshops. Caves and rock shelters were still inhabited in neolithic times as they had been in palæolithic. More frequently, however, neolithic man preferred to dwell in the open. His whole industry and outlook on life suggests that he was the child of forest clearings. He built therefore what is usually known as pit dwellings.

A hole in the ground was dug about four feet deep and ten to twelve feet across, and the earth heaped up round it to a height of three or four feet. The top was probably covered with boughs heaped over with earth, a framework of wood having been first erected to support the superstructure, and a small hole left for the door. This type of dwelling is not altogether unknown among modern primitive peoples. The geographical surroundings essential for such a dwelling are a comparatively light sandy soil which can easily be dug, and the presence of suitable timber to bear the superstructure.

Those of us who lived in dug-outs of a not dissimilar nature during the war can testify to the comfort which can be obtained in such surroundings with a careful choice of ground. Where soil was not available owing to the rocky nature of the ground, its place was taken by stone built in dry courses.

The most remarkable of the neolithic dwellings are probably of rather a later date, namely, the pile-dwellings or palafittes. The size of these may be judged from the fact that the largest one at Roben-hausen has been estimated to cover an area of 120,000 square feet. These dwellings were made by driving into the bed of the lake piles which were roughly pointed with an implement and then hardened in the fire. A number of stages were erected side by side on these long piles. Platforms were made by laying beams, brushwood and earth on the stages, and a house was made between two stages, the upper forming the roof and the latter the floor. A skirting was made by forcing a plank edgewise between two horizontally laid boards. In the centre of the house a fireplace was built of stones and clay. There were gangways which could be raised or lowered, connecting the village with the mainland. The immense amount of labour and organization which are required to build such a village testify to the degree of civilization which these people had reached.

The lakes have preserved some of the textiles which these people had in use. It is clear that they were acquainted with the loom, and that although they did not know of hemp they used flax. It is worthy of note that they did not use the present cultivated species of flax, but a wild species common in Europe to-day, *Linum angustifolium*.

They seem to have practised a good deal of trade from the distribution of their artefacts. The dwellers on the sea-coast must have been acquainted at least with the elements of navigation from the bones of fish which remain to show that they ventured off shore.

The largest dug-out which has survived was one found on Lake Chalain, which measured nearly nine and a half metres long and had a beam of three-quarters of a metre, about two feet six inches.

It will be seen from these outlines that the material culture of neolithic man was high. Many of the greatest developments did not take place till bronze was, if not in general use, at least widely known in some parts of the world. At this stage we must leave the study of prehistoric man. His next developments gave him the right which the modern archæologists must accord to him of being civilized. We must remember that in classical lands the memory of the Bronze Age lingered on and was not forgotten in a time which gave us some of the greatest treasures of European literature.

If we turn to modern savages we shall find many things which are much more primitive and indeed often remind us of the older Stone Age. Other things again seem to be much more advanced. Culture can seldom be kept in water-tight compartments, and even the remotest savage cannot help being affected by what is happening in the world around him.

CHAPTER X

LABOUR ON THE TUNDRA

Chukchee and Samoyed

IN the last two chapters we have been dealing with the progress of labour in early times. Our studies have necessarily been confined to Western Europe, and owing often to lack of evidence it has been necessary to supplement our meagre knowledge with conjecture or with references to what appear to be parallel cases among modern primitive peoples. In what follows we are better prepared. Travellers have studied modern primitive peoples, and examples of the products of their labours can be found in museums. It is possible therefore to make a fairly complete picture of their methods of life. For convenience of reference the same arrangement has been followed as in Chapter V, that is, first the dwellers in the tundra of the north have been described. We have then followed a southerly course, passing through the various climatic zones until tropical forests and the clearings of those forests are reached.

The dwellers in the Arctic tundras of Northern Asia present problems of special interest to all students of primitive peoples. They have been recently most carefully studied by various members of the Jesup Expedition, and in the following pages I have depended almost entirely on the sumptuous volumes in which

the results of the expedition are recorded, and especially
on the volume by Bogoras on the Chukchee.

The Chukchee are of special interest as they
represent a tribe which lives in a very unsatisfactory
environment and at the same time so successfully, at
least as far as some parts of the tribe are concerned, that
many even of the more advanced peoples are at times
dependent on them in times of scarcity. They are
also of interest for our present purpose because their
culture, which is not very old, seems to be in the
course of transition from that of pure hunters to that
of pastoral nomads. They may be conveniently
divided into two groups, the maritime and the reindeer Chukchee. Most of the following discussion
concerns the latter people. The villages of the
maritime Chukchee are situated on the Arctic coast
beyond East Cape and on the coast of the Bering Sea
between that Cape and Anadyr Bay. The reindeer
camps are scattered over the whole of the country to
the north-east of a line drawn from the mouth of the
Indighirka River to Cape Anannon.

The region is for the most part tundra, but it
extends as far as the northern limits of the forest.
There are certain well-marked climatic differences
between the various regions. In the Kolyma district
birch trees are well developed as far north as 69°, and
willows are found even further to the north. The
country is generally cold and dry. On the Pacific
coast, however, the snowfall is heavier, and the chief
trees are willow and poplar. In the river valleys
almost everywhere very stunted willows and alders
are found. The coast, however, presents a very
desolate appearance; for many miles reindeer moss
and a few lichens are the only forms of vegetable
growth, otherwise the whole area is bare and

desolate.   On sandy spots there is so little grass
that the people who depend on it for the soles of their
boots have to travel inland to obtain it.

The villages on this bare coast are on the whole
mobile, depending as they do on seal hunting. The
reindeer camps are usually built along the rivers, the
normal situation for any primitive dwelling. They
are usually built in groups, and when the autumn
comes on they seek the shelter of the forest to protect
them from the blizzards of the Arctic winter. They
usually remain on the edge of the forest and do not
penetrate because of the difficulty that the big-horned
reindeer experience in a forest. At the approach of
spring the herds are driven on to the tundra, often
as far as the coast in order to avoid the plague of all
herds, swarms of insects. Like all nomadic peoples
they usually keep to their own territory, though they
may travel over a district of considerable size, even as
far as 150 miles.

The most distinctive feature of the arts of life of
these peoples is the domestication of the reindeer. It
does not appear that they have been in possession of
reindeer for a long time, and it is possible that these
very distinctive reindeer people only learned the use
of the reindeer by culture-contact, as there appears to
be certain differences in the type of deer from that used
by the more westerly peoples. They may even have
learned to tame the wild deer. Bogoras draws a very
instructive comparison between the various types of
reindeer breeders. Among the tribes on the western
shores of the Arctic Sea, as for instance the Lapps,
the Zyrians and the Samoyeds, the economic life is
not unlike that of cattle breeders. They use the deer
as our ancestors used the ox. Their existence depends
on the supply of meat and skins which the herd

supplies. Their methods of caring for the herds are fairly uniform, and almost all use the dog to guard the herd. The deer are thoroughly domesticated; they are harnessed to sledges and are used for food, including milk.

The Tungus and Lamuts of Eastern Siberia have less well tamed herds, although they have them sufficiently under control to milk them. The most remarkable part of their culture is that they ride and do not drive their animals, a method which is mentioned by Marco Polo. Their dogs are still the natural enemies of the reindeer, and they are kept tied up or they will hunt the herds. These dogs are used for hunting only. These people are not truly nomadic, but the possession of the herds very considerably adds to the range of their hunting and fishing grounds. Their herds on the whole are small and therefore are not used for food except where there is a surplus of animals. They are reserved purely for transport.

These people then are clearly only on the verge of passing from the hunting stage to the stage of pastoral nomadism. East and north of the Tungus, however, the Koryak and the Chukchee possess very large herds. They represent a very imperfect stage of domestication, and it is impossible to milk the deer. The dogs are very wild and are used for hunting not herding. The deer are difficult to manage even in harness. These people also represent a transitional stage even less developed, as they can hardly be said to do much more than to follow semi-wild herds and to select for breaking-in such young animals as seem most promising.

They are therefore by no means so dependent on the reindeer as some of the more advanced tribes. Some of them combine seal hunting and reindeer breeding.

Part of a tribe lives in huts on the coast hunting and fishing, thus making a maritime village. Another part wanders inland up in the mountains with the reindeer. Most of the fishermen possess reindeer who will be under the care of a member of the family, so that there will be a continuous communication between the people who happen to be living on the shore and those who are with the herds.

The herds are always on the move; they cannot remain long in one place because the constant scraping of the ground with their hoofs hardens the snow. They feed in winter on the reindeer moss (*Cetraria*) which grows on the tundra, and in summer they eat the sprouting vegetation of that barren land. Their herdsmen have acquired some skill in breeding, and they constantly strengthen the strain by crossing with wild deer, a matter sometimes of some difficulty, as the breeding season of the two is slightly different. They have to contend with the carnivorous enemies of the deer, especially the wolverine, the polar wolf and the bear. The wolves are sometimes caught with the lasso made of sealskin which is normally used for catching the reindeer.

The possession of these herds, wild as they are, adds very much to the stability of the existence of these peoples. Most of the tribes who depend entirely on seal hunting and fishing are often on the verge of starvation, and some of the fisherfolk in the Kolyma district, who appear to be generally in a higher stage of culture, are dependent on the Chukchee for skins and for clothing.

The food of the Chukchee shows very clearly both the effect of environment, the demand made by the excessively cold polar climate, and the result of their traditional culture. Their staple food is animal, a condition which contrasts very strongly with some of the primitive hunting peoples of tropical forests who seem to prefer to subsist mainly on vegetable products.

Not only do the Chukchee prefer animal food, but they prefer that which has the highest fat content, and they seem to have a marked craving for blubber. Both divisions of the people, reindeer and maritime, are said to prefer the meat of sea-mammals. The reason that they give is that it was the food of their ancestors; the higher fat content may also be an important factor. The flesh of the reindeer, however, naturally bulks as the most important article of diet among the reindeer people, and those living on the sea-shore eat it with pleasure, both because of its taste and because of the change in diet. Blood is a very important part of their diet, and is eaten in any condition, raw or fermenting or putrid.

Their methods of preparing food are extremely revolting. They consider that meat, raw and frozen hard, is as palatable as that which has been cooked, although at present most of their food is boiled. The liver, kidneys, tendons and marrow of the reindeer are eaten raw immediately after slaughter. They will eat the flesh that is half putrid with maggots, and even worse forms of diet. On the sea coast where fuel is very rare more raw food is eaten. The Chukchee eat animals who have died of disease, and even those sea animals which drift ashore.

Little effort is made to preserve any meat; it is true that a small portion is dried, but this drying is very carelessly done, and most of the provisions seem, unless frozen, to be in a semi-putrid state. Blubber they do keep in bags, but it is not chewed as among some other peoples.

This disgusting form of diet seems to form their

staple food. They do not entirely avoid vegetable food, but Bogoras states that they use it rather as a substitute in times of scarcity of meat than as a regular change from meat diet. The importance of at least a small amount of vegetable food in a normal diet seems, however, to suggest that vegetables also, at least to a certain extent, are eaten because of the physiological craving of the body. Moss is extracted from the paunch of the reindeer and is boiled with blood, fat and chopped collops. The leaves of the willow and the bark is also used. These vegetables are also mixed with blood and boiled to a thick soup. The maritime people store them for winter use. A pudding made out of tallow, the choicest bits of meat and roots is considered a most delicious dish, but they also eat roots raw, this form of vegetable being the only one which they relish. The roots are gathered by the women, who in general appear to use more vegetable food than the men.

Their bill of fare is a monotonous one. The staple dish is boiled meat, the brisket being considered the best joint. They use brick tea in enormous quantities; they have no milk and practically no sugar. Their principal meal is in the evening, when they eat ravenously.

One or two of the abnormalities of their diet are interesting. They sometimes mix a kind of white clay with their broth. Pitch from the larch tree is used as chewing-gum, and the Eskimo and the coast Chukchee make a preparation of seal oil which they boil from the dregs until it is ductile and sticky. Tobacco is widely used, and a tobacco famine is severely felt. Their only stimulant is the fly agaric, a kind of fungus which they eat with the result that they develop an advanced condition of intoxication.

The use of this drug is comparatively limited owing to the fact that it does not grow outside the limits of the forest. Its use is therefore more common among the Koryak than among the Chukchee.

I have alluded to the important part which the reindeer plays in their culture. Hunting is, however, very generally practised among the coastal people especially. Their methods may be briefly summarized. Seal hunting forms the most important pursuit of the coastal people. They catch them either by sitting at a blow hole and waiting till the seal comes up to breathe, or by stalking, or by the use of nets. When stalking they wear an ingenious cap which is made to look like the head of a seal. For catching fish they use nets, and they also angle, both in the rivers and in the sea. The reindeer people often do not get much chance of catching fish when they are up in the mountains with the herds.

In modern days they use old guns for shooting game, but they, like all savages, are past-masters in the art of snaring. They use a trap which has a bow ready set. When the animal springs the trap a spear is driven into it. They also use the sling, the bolas, and various forms of snares. One of the most ingenious of their devices is a spit of whalebone which is bound up with sinew and imbedded in a bait. The animal which swallows this has his intestines pierced by the sharp whalebone as the sinew dissolves in the stomach. This instrument is widely spread among Arctic peoples.

Generally speaking, the Chukchee habitation consists of a large round skin tent which in winter forms the dwelling-room. The outside of this tent and the form in many suggests the yurt, which in its familiar form has been so highly developed by the nomads of

Central Asia. Among the reindeer Chukchee the framework consists of three large poles which are tied together as a tripod. This frame is then elaborated by the addition of further stakes. The whole forms an elastic framework which is weighted down with stones, a custom which is still retained in the Mongol "yurt." The framework is covered with a skin cover. They normally use an old cover in the summer and a new one in winter.

The inner tent is practically a little box. It is about four and a half feet high by seven feet by twelve. It is supported on two horizontal poles, the rear ends of which are fastened to the framework and the front are supported on forked sticks.

All this elaborate paraphernalia is of course very heavy, and makes up six or seven sledge loads. The herdsmen therefore carry a light sleeping-room or tent. When the family migrate to the forest at the beginning of the winter they make a special semi-permanent dwelling. This consists of three parts. In front there is an entrance room, which is made of a few stakes and an old tent cover. Secondly, they erect a main tent in the usual way, but they use an old cover lest a new cover should be damaged by the fire which is kept burning inside continually. The sleeping-room is usually larger.

In addition the reindeer Chukchee often build a kind of annexe in the forest. This is made of wood and is of a simple conical shape. It is used for tallow boiling. The maritime Chukchee suffer from a shortage of poles, so that they often build the walls of sods. They usually use an old cover bought from the reindeer Chukchee. Cellars are used and made for storing. In the old days the people seem to have made underground dwellings.

This type of house is of great interest because it stands as a primitive type of house which has evolved in two different directions. Among the Mongols the general form can still be recognized. The framework has become more elaborate. Instead of lashed stakes the walls are now made with a lattice which can be folded, and the house has become more portable. The outer cover is now made of felt, which is not as warm as skins but more easy to handle and to mend. The tent is still secured in position by stones tied to ropes which hold the yurt in place. The inner tent has disappeared, but the herdsmen when they travel take with them a little tent with a ridge pole, which is rapidly transported.

Among the Navajo a very different line of evolution has taken place, the tent has become less mobile instead of more mobile. The parallel with these latter people is of particular interest, because it seems probable that the Chukchee represent a backwash into Asia from the American continent, and the Navajo are Athapascan and therefore connected at least linguistically with the Indians of the north-west. Their hogans, as they call their dwellings, are very much of the same shape, that is, they have walls which incline slightly inwards and have a low roof on the top with a hole for the smoke to escape.

It would seem at first sight that the resemblance ends there, but if the construction of many of the hogans be examined it will be seen that the principle of the architecture of the two is similar, but in the case of the hogans the cover is now of wood, especially where pignon is available or in default of this earth and brush. A very much more solid and permanent house has been obtained at the expense of mobility, and the people are therefore compelled to build houses

at various places on the route of their annual
migrations.

The house of the Chukchee contains little furniture.
The people either lie flat on their stomachs or sit cross-
legged on the floor which is covered with skins. The
most important article of furniture in the inner room
is the lamp, which gives both light and heat. The
reindeer Chukchee use a small round lamp made of
clay or soapstone, although to-day these primitive
appliances have for the most part been superseded by
an old saucepan and a wooden bowl covered with sheet-
iron. The lamp is usually placed in a shallow wooden
bowl which stands on a tray, and in some cases the
bowl and tray are of one piece. A wick is made of
sphagnum moss, and blubber or reindeer tallow is
used as fuel, the bowl serving to catch the drippings.
The maritime peoples and the Asiatic Eskimo use a
rather larger lamp of clay.

The old women remember the time when kettles of
clay were used. These kettles were not baked but
were well dried before the fire after being coated with
seal or reindeer blood. At the present time iron
kettles are used. Of the domestic utensils the bone-
breaking set is the most important possession of the
tribes, especially among the reindeer people. It
includes several stone hammers, a large flat stone on
which the bones are laid, and a flat cylindrical con-
tainer of walrus hide which is used to hold the broken
bones. The hammer is oblong and is grooved down
the middle. A short handle is firmly lashed to it.

The water supply is a difficult and important
question among all Arctic peoples, especially in winter.
Snow is put in a kettle under which a wooden dish is
placed to catch the drippings. This kettle is put in
front of the fire at night in the inner tent, and is

often spilled by somebody moving in his sleep. The other domestic utensils include wooden dishes, drinking tubes which are made from the leg bones of a swan, and sealskin bags which are used for storing meat and clothes.

The clothing of the Chukchee consists of reindeer skins with the hair inside. Three garments are worn—a long tunic, breeches and high boots.

This brief survey will show the manner of life of the nomads of the tundras. It must be remembered, as has been stated above, that their culture in spite of its primitive nature is not a very ancient one, and that the time is probably not very distant when they were hunters. It is for this very reason that their culture is of special interest, showing as it does the transition from hunting to pastoral nomadism. For comparative purposes it may be convenient to describe briefly the Samoyeds who live to the west of the Chukchee and have many features in common with them.

The Samoyeds also are mainly dependent on the reindeer. Montefiore[1] states that they know little of vegetables and that they care less, a statement that is probably exaggerated. When they are camped near rivers they catch fish, and in the summer they eat geese when they can catch them. They seem to have the same passion for blood which is so characteristic of all Arctic tribes. It is stated that they will open the vein of a live deer and drink the blood and then close it again. Their habitations differ from those of the Chukchee in certain interesting ways. The framework of the tent is made of twenty poles varying in thickness; they are about sixteen feet long and are

[1] Montefiore, " The Samoyeds of the Great Tundra," Journ. Roy. Anthrop. Instit., XXIV (1894), p. 400.

lashed together near the top. They are then twisted and opened out.

In the summer strips of birch bark about eighteen inches wide are lashed over the framework. These strips are first softened by being boiled, and then are sewn together by stout threads made of sinew. In the winter the covering is made of skins, usually reindeer and foxes—in the old days bear was used, but to-day bearskins seem to be too valuable for this purpose. The inside of this tent, or choom as they call it, is hung with further skins. The top for about eighteen inches has no covering, and the space thus left open serves as a chimney. About three feet from the ground a light pole is fixed transversely across the choom, the two ends being lashed to the vertical frame poles. A big hook is fastened to this, which serves to suspend the cooking-pot. The interior tent seems to be absent, otherwise the resemblance is great.

The clothing is similar; all are clothed in reindeer skins. The men wear a tunic made with the hair inside; the garment reaches to the knees, but in the cold weather it is girded up so as to leave a large and baggy air space, which provides addition warmth. Deer-skin breeches are worn and boots of the same material with sealskin soles; these boots reach as high as the knees. In very cold weather another tunic is put on top of the first. Over the tunic or tunics a belt is worn to hold a sheath-knife, a calculating stick and a snuff-box. The dress of the women does not differ materially from that of the men, except that their tunic is open in front.

CHAPTER XI

LABOUR IN NORTHERN FORESTS

Gilyak and Ainu

THE people who have been described in the previous pages are true tundra-dwellers who migrate to the forest only to secure the necessary shelter from the Arctic winter. As an example of the primitive forest-dweller, akin possibly in some of the elements of his culture to the early inhabitants of some of the deciduous forests of Europe, I have chosen the Gilyaks. They inhabit the lower course of the Amur river and the northern part of Saghalien, and are partly fishermen and partly hunters, and live under very severe climatic conditions. They catch fish either with nets or with the rod and line. The nets are made of nettle or wild hemp with wooden netting needles, an occupation which normally belongs to the women. Sea-mammals are sometimes killed with a harpoon. They follow the larger deer on snow-shoes and kill them with a spear. Their principal weapon is, however, the bow. They use both a simple bow and one that is made up and backed with horn and sinew. They feather their arrows and usually fit them with iron points. As is usual, however, among so many peoples, they often kill birds with blunted arrows. Their game includes most of the wild mammals which live in the region—foxes, pigs, sables, bear, reindeer and other deer.

In spite of this diversity of game, however, they do not use meat as their principal article of diet, although bear and reindeer are considered delicacies. The principal food is fish, and includes among other varieties, sturgeon, carp, smelt, salmon and trout. The freshly caught fish is eaten raw and in winter it is frozen. In the summer fish that is not required is dried. They eat, as all the northern peoples, seal blubber and the flesh of sea-mammals, and in case of need will even eat their dogs. They collect the eggs of wild birds at the right season of the year.

The Gilyaks appear to use more vegetable food than the Chukchee. They collect and eat a good deal of the wild garlic. They make considerable use of wild berries, some of which are eaten with seal blubber. To-day they also buy millet from the Chinese.

In addition to the bow and nets mentioned above, the Gilyaks possess a knife which is not unlike that used by the Eskimo. It is short-bladed and has the end of the wooden handle cut with a bevel for the thumb. They also use thong drills with iron points for boring holes. Their domestic utensils are made either of wood or more frequently of birch bark. Most of their food is eaten raw, but they cook what may be described as porridge and soup. They chew a piece of dried fish and when it is soft they put it into a birch-bark basket. All is then collected into a vessel and mixed with meat, berries, cedar-nuts, flour, and seal blubber, and boiled till it becomes a kind of thick soup. They drink this and their vegetable porridge from wooden saucers.

The houses of the Gilyaks differ in summer and winter, and there is also a slight difference between those on Saghalien and on the mainland. The winter houses are built in the forest, usually near a river.

There may be as few as three or as many as twelve huts together. They are partly excavated in the ground. The floor is made of earth or clay stamped hard, and the roof of dried grass mixed with earth. The whole is usually strengthened with stones. The main structure is built of timber, of which there is naturally no lack, and is stable. In some cases they made windows which are glazed with fish skins. Inside, like the Chukchee, they not infrequently have an inner room, made of pine timbers with an earthen hearth in the middle, where the water-pot is kept. In some houses they have an arrangement for letting out the smoke, which is like that of the Golds and the Manchus, and, in a modified form, the Chinese. The smoke is conducted under raised benches and thus helps to warm the hut.

In the summer they build lighter dwellings, simple log huts of fir or willow with birch-bark roofs. These huts are usually placed in relation to the fishing grounds.

The dress of the Gilyak is the same in both sexes, and differs in summer and in winter. In the former at present for the most part they wear the cotton cloth which they buy from the traders. In winter they make their clothes from sealskin, or failing that from dogskin. The actual garments are similar to those of most of Northern Asia, and consist of a long tunic, trousers and high boots. I once saw several of these people thus clad at Hakodate in Northern Japan, and in their rough furs they presented a very strange contrast to the rest of the daintily, and, for the weather, inadequately clad Japanese crowd.

The Gilyaks have well-developed means of transportation. In the winter they use long wooden snow-shoes, not unlike very broad skis. For carrying things they have light wooden sledges drawn by dogs. They have several kinds of boats, including large dug-outs made of fir or cedar wood and lighter canoes made of birch bark. At present the Chinese are developing a trade with these people, as they have done for so long among all the primitive peoples of Eastern Asia.

These primitive hunters are the near neighbours of a tribe who since they first became known to European scientists have always excited their interest, the Ainu. These latter people live partly in the northern island of Japan (Hokkaido) and partly in Saghalien. There is a certain amount of difference in the cultures of the two branches; the following description refers to the Hokkaido group.[1] A great deal of change has come over them within the last generation owing to advance of Japanese colonists all over the island. The home of the Ainu in this region lies in a cold, bleak and dismal land. Their villages are either along the coast or near rivers, a situation which in the old days assured the easy capture of game. The country is compara-tively mountainous, but the shores are often low and desolate. The people themselves have many peculiar-ities. With their long and flowing beards and the lighter colour of their skins and the complete absence of a slanting eye they present a very strong contrast with the Japanese who are occupying their old hunting grounds.

Considerable alterations in their modes of life, due to the Japanese restrictions of their hunting and fishing rights, combined with the presence of Japanese trade goods, make it somewhat difficult at present to recon-struct their old culture in its pure form. The most

[1] I am indebted to Dr. Batchelor for much of what follows, both for the accounts that he has published of the Ainu and still more for the personal introduction that he gave me to the Ainu, and for the hospitality he showed me in Hokkaido.

important features, however, seem to have been somewhat as follows.   At present they are coming to
depend more and more on vegetable food, which they
complained had a very serious effect on their digestions.
In the old days they were mostly meat eaters, although
they did practise a certain amount of primitive
agriculture.   Their position in fact closely parallels
that of the Chukchee.   The former are developing
from a hunting into a stage of reindeer nomadism.
The Ainu, on the other hand, were developing from
the hunting stage to that of agriculture, a development
that is being considerably hurried by the Japanese.

A generation ago bear, deer and other animals,
salmon and many kinds of fish were exceedingly
abundant, and formed the greater part of their food.
Deer were hunted by stalking and also by packs of
dogs.   They also possessed an ingenious arrangement
for decoying the deer.   They have a musical
instrument which when they blow it makes a noise
like a fawn and so attracts the deer.   Bears they used
to hunt with bows and arrows, spears and pit-traps.
It is claimed that the Ainu hunters would attack the
bear in his den, but the evidence for such daring is
based on the tales of the hunters themselves.

Their principal weapon in all their hunting was the
bow and arrow.   The bow was a simple instrument
of wood.   The arrow was more complicated.   It consisted of three parts, a shaft made of reed, a piece of
bone which formed a neck between the shaft and the
head, and a head made of bamboo which is scooped out
to hold poison.   The poison usually used for the
arrows was either a vegetable substance such as aconite
or arisæma, or made from the body of a kind of water
scorpion.   The traps which they use are adaptations
of the bow.   They use a spring bow with a line

attached, which the passing animal catches with its foot. The bow is then released and sets free the arrow, which transfixes the animal. A second type using the bow principle catches the animal by the foot, as do the majority of our spring traps. Rats are caught by ingenious small traps which also operate on the bow principle. In these an arrow is shot or else a kind of box is closed by the springing of the bow, thus confining the animal.

The most important fish that the Ainu caught was the salmon. They used a spear about eight feet long. To the end of the spear they fastened a hook in such a way that when the fish was struck the hook entered the flesh and pulled the fish between it and the end of the pole. Thus the more the fish struggled the more firmly it became embedded and held, and the better the purchase of the fisherman became. Fishing was usually done from the river bank, but the Ainu also fished for salmon from boats. In the late autumn they used to fish with torch-light. Before the Japanese restricted their fishing rights they used to use nets made of hemp and of fibre of mugwort (*Artemisia*).

In some streams they made fish-traps. Stakes were driven into the river-bed and the space between was enclosed with wickerwork. A narrow entrance was left in the middle, where the fishermen fastened a net. When the fish arrived at the end of the trap and were in the net, one end of it was raised by the fisherman and so the fish was caught. Mud-trout and pike were caught with a double spear, to the end of which iron points were fastened. In order to attract the fish a piece of iron was wrapped in blue material and the whole was bound with white bark. This was dragged through the water. For the larger fish and marine mammals, such as sharks, swordfish and sea-lions, the Ainu used to use harpoons.

All these occupations were essentially the work of the men, and represent a fairly typical hunting stage of culture. Side by side with this, however, the women practised agriculture, and under present con-ditions, with the restrictions on hunting and fishing, this work of the women has an ever increasing import-ance. Their principal crops are barley, millet, beans, potatoes and peas. The women get up while it is still dark and often exceedingly bleak and cold, eat some cold vegetable broth and some raw dried fish. Then they go to their gardens or to the fields and gather the wild grasses of which their house walls are built, or to work in their gardens. These are small patches of land which are situated either on the banks of some stream or in a tiny sheltered valley. They cultivate each garden for two or three years and then let it go to waste. The method of reaping their crops is to pinch off the ears with a bit of shell. They also make use of wild plants.

In the autumn they collect chestnuts, and they gather the roots of *Erythronium dens canis*, the dog-tooth violet, which they wash, boil, mash and make into cakes.

Their methods of preparing food have been much affected by culture-contact with the Japanese. Pottery is apparently unknown among the Ainu, and the pots which they use at present are all Japanese. Consider-able stress has been laid on this absence of pots, especially among writers on Japanese archæology. Excavations which have been recently carried out show the presence of a type of culture which may be generally described as neolithic; that is to say that it is a Stone Age culture, using polished stone implements but no metals. One of the strongest arguments that has been put forward for the culture not being Ainu is that these people used pottery.

It is very dangerous to argue from physique to culture, but after a careful examination of the crania and other human remains I was quite unable to distinguish them from those of the Ainu, nor did the arguments put forward by the excavators convince me that such differences as appeared were other than superficial. If these neolithic people are the ancestors of the modern Ainu, and their physique would suggest a very close similarity, we have here an example of a people who once having known the use of pottery have abandoned its manufacture. Such a hypothesis is doubtful, and must remain unconfirmed until we have further evidence.

At present all that can be said is that the Ainu seem to be entirely ignorant of the manufacture of pots, although they readily buy and use those made by the Japanese. Their own vessels are made of wood or bark. For boiling they use very flimsy containers made of the bark of cherry, although their use is almost obsolete. These saucepans are filled with vegetables. Most of their household gear is made of wood. They use wooden trays, spoons and mortars. The millet is threshed in the mortar and subsequently beaten out into a kind of flour or paste, which they cook into what looks and tastes like a semolina pudding. At present this seems to be a very important part of their diet, although in the old days it certainly played a secondary part and was used chiefly in times of scarcity. A characteristic implement of every Ainu household is a long piece of wood which is used by the men for raising the moustache when drinking in order that it may not touch the liquid. They are at present very prone to drunkenness, the liquor they usually use being imported Japanese *sake*.

In the old days fire was made by rubbing together two bits of elm root. Subsequently they borrowed the use of the flint and steel from the Japanese, and to-day they have the cheap Japanese matches which have such a wide distribution as trade goods over so much of Eastern Asia. A fire is usually kept up in the middle of the house in an open hearth. Over this fire there hangs a large wooden frame from which kettles are suspended. Although they are thus well provided with means of preparing food, much of their cooking remains elementary. Their fish is cleaned, smoked and dried. It is frequently eaten raw, and they depend quite a lot on sea foods which are not elaborately prepared. The eggs of fish form an important dish when obtainable, and they have a special mortar which they use for mashing up salmon roes.

The Ainu huts represent a particularly interesting development. The previous houses which we have discussed in the far north have always been very mobile in their structure. They have been planned to keep out the cold and at the same time to be placed on sledges and moved to another situation. The Ainu, on the other hand, have villages which are clearly intended to be permanent, and this in spite of the fact that the hunting stage had been by no means permanently abandoned. This may be accounted for partly by the fact that the game in the old days was very abundant and that their villages were built near where there was always likely to be game; secondly, they also have always been fishermen, a condition which makes, as I have shown, for permanence of habitation; and thirdly, the fact that, although they could hardly be called agriculturalists, yet agriculture had reached the

stage of being a permanent part of their economic
life.

The Ainu begin by building their house at the roof.
They lash the rafters to long ridge poles at one end;
the other end of these rafters being tied to horizontal
poles. The framework thus made is strengthened by
smaller poles, and over these again a thatch is made
out of wild grasses.[1] They usually use bast or vines
to make the lashings. When the roof is complete
magnolia poles about the height of a man are driven
into the ground, four or five feet apart. To these
smaller poles are lashed, and the walls thus made are
thatched. These uprights are cut with a fork at the
top, and when the thatching is complete the roof is
lifted into place. Two holes are usually left in the
thatch of the walls for windows, and a kind of clerestory
is made below the ridge poles so that the smoke can
find its way out.

A porch is built at the west end. This forms a kind
of antechamber where boots are left. The floor is
raised about two feet and is made of polished boards.
The visitor climbs from the porch on to this floor.
The interior contains the fireplace which I have already
described, and under the eaves there are little spaces
which are used for sleeping places, except for the
master and mistress, who sleep by the fire.
The corner on the left opposite the door usually
forms a repository, in the recess under the eaves, for
the family heirlooms and treasures. To-day a great
many of these are Japanese. This type of house has
progressed a long way from that of the Chukchee.

[1] It is of importance to note that the Ainu method of
building the roof differs fundamentally from that of the
Japanese. Professor Cholnoky has drawn my attention to
the similarity which exists between the Ainu method and
that of some of the aboriginal tribes of Western China.

The fact that they build the roof first seems alone to recall that the origin of these complex dwellings was in all probability a tent.

Outside the porch and separate from it the Ainu usually build a small storehouse on piles. This store does not differ essentially in construction from the house except for the piles, which are put there to protect the stores from the attacks of rodents and other marauders.

The clothing of the Ainu also shows a great contrast from the other peoples described in the last chapter. They make fibre out of elm bark, from which their stuffs are woven. The bark is stripped and put into water till it is thoroughly soft. It is then pulled out and made into balls of thread. If it is to be used for sewing it is chewed before being wound. The yarn is often dyed by being immersed first in a solution of oak bark and then in marshy places where there is an abundance of iron in the water. The fibre is woven into a cloth on a loom in which the alternate threads are separated by a frame with either three or four bars, not unlike the reel that is used by ourselves for winding rope. The cloth is cut and sewn into garments which are often elaborately embroidered, with different patterns according to the sex of the wearer. In winter these bark clothes are made warmer by skins being sewn on to them.

The Ainu wear gloves which protect the back of the hands but not the palms. Their legs are protected by a kind of gaiter which is made of wild grasses or of reeds. In the winter they sometimes use snow-shoes. In summer they either go barefoot, or if they are going to make a long journey they have sandals which are made of the tough bark of the vine.

Although a few ponies are sometimes to be seen in

the Ainu villages, both their agriculture and their transportation are limited except by water to the women. The latter will carry very heavy loads for long periods, supporting the weight by a band which passes over the forehead.

Boats are naturally of importance to any sea-going people. The river boats are made of hollowed out logs. The sea-going boats have a stem made of a heavy piece of wood to which planks are stitched clinkerwise and sewn with thread made from the bark of the elm—the same kind of thread in fact which they use for sewing their garments. The wood used is usually oak. The boats have a broad stern, and are propelled by a pole in shallow water and by oars in deep water. These boats are used for fishing both in the sea and in rivers.

This brief survey will show that in spite of adverse geographical conditions the Ainu have advanced to a state of culture which is relatively high. They have permanent homes; they practise a primitive form of agriculture; they no longer use merely skins for their clothing but know the use of the loom. In spite of this fact, in many ways they are extremely primitive, and may be said to represent perhaps the final stage of primitive life before it definitely develops into barbarism.

CHAPTER XII

LABOUR IN PLAINS AND DESERTS

ALTHOUGH in many respects the inhabitants of the great steppes of Asia have long since passed from the primitive stage of development, yet in other ways they may be said to be the most typical of the nomads whose existence depends on the horse. These peoples have a wide distribution, and have at one time or another during the course of human history dominated the whole of the grass lands which stretch almost from the Pacific shores into Europe.

From these scattered tribes there have at times risen other groups, slightly more civilized than their neighbours, who have become the founders of great but often short-lived military aristocracies. The most famous of these is probably that which was founded by the Mongols under Ghenghis Khan, who was succeeded by his even more famous grandson, Kublai Khan. We are fortunate in possessing excellent accounts from mediaeval travellers of these people. Marco Polo has given us a tale which in its vividness and wealth of detail is surpassed among travellers' tales only by Herodotus. Rubriquis and Carpini crossed Asia, and they too have added greatly to our knowledge of these wild barbarians who have exercised so profound an influence on the imagination of the West since first they were known.

Except for the fact that they are now dominated by

Buddhism, which has had a profound effect on all their methods of life, the material culture of the Mongols does not seem to be very different from what it was when we first hear accounts of them. Their culture is so closely related to their environment, and they seem within certain limits to possess so stable a material culture, that they may be conveniently taken as representing the ultimate development of pastoral nomadism.

They are in extremely close relation to the country in which they live. The horse, their principal domestic animal, is a native of Central Asia. Their other domestic animals are also to be found in the same region. Although they have made considerable progress, there is little in their life, except the very alien Buddhism, which does not recall the plains over which they wander. Even the old animistic beliefs which have preceded Buddhism survive in a limited degree, and they sacrifice sheep before their rude altars and perform other Shamanistic rites which belong to the culture which they possessed before they accepted the alien religion.

The country in which the Mongols live is typically grass-land; in places it becomes barren and practically desert. In other places there are mountains and babbling brooks. In the greater part of their home, however, there is abundant pasturage for their herds, and at the same time such a lack of timber that a few stunted bushes in a sheltered valley are a sight which the traveller may ride miles to see. The climate is continental and extreme. In the winter the ground is frozen and covered with snow, and subject to the effects of an almost Arctic blizzard. The spring is comparatively short, and with the coming of summer the grass is soon dried and browned.

Any people therefore who are dependent on nature rather than on their crops are compelled to wander far, according to the season, in order to find pasturage for their animals and to get water and shelter for themselves. The food quest for the Mongols is limited practically entirely to the products of their herds. The chief domestic animal is the pony. These ponies seem to be very closely akin to Prejvalsky's horse, the wild horse of Central Asia, whose remains are found in cave deposits of Europe and whose portrait has been so graphically drawn by cave artists. At present, as far as I know, the horse is not eaten, but mare's milk is of great importance, especially as a basis for fermented liquors. At the time of year that the mares are with their foals, every Mongol of position always has mares tied up outside his tent to provide for any guests who may arrive.

Although the camels form such a prominent feature of all the trading caravans they are not to be seen in any great numbers, and, indeed, often not at all off the trade routes. They should therefore rather be discussed in relation to trade than in relation to the food quest.

Sheep and goats form an important part of the wealth of every village. They provide the milk, which in a semi-rancid and buttery state is put into the tea and is also made into cheese. Mutton is an important article of diet. It is usual on any great occasion to roast a sheep whole, and after a wedding the bride's father usually sends her several sheep roasted in this way to show that she is not dependent on her new relations for food. That mutton should be thus sent ceremonially proves, I am inclined to think, the importance which the Mongols themselves attach to it as an article of diet.

In some cases the Mongols do cultivate small patches of land, but this is alien to their true culture, and therefore beyond our present purpose. Most of them, however, do obtain grain, which they make into very hard cakes which are eaten with cheese. They also make the grain into a kind of porridge. Brick tea is obtained by the usual channels of trade, and is inseparable from their meals.

In places where game is plentiful, and this is true of most of Mongolia, except possibly parts of Gobi, they are skilful hunters. There can be little doubt that the principal weapon of the Mongols is the bow. Their weapon is made of horn backed by sinew, of the type technically known as " composite." It is overstrung, that is to say that in making the bow it is so moulded that the belly of the bow when unstrung is directed backwards instead of forwards as it is when the bow is strung. The surface of the bow is often elaborately decorated, although the horn is usually left bare. Blunted arrows are sometimes used for shooting birds. Although sometimes to-day crossbows are used, these are almost certainly imported from China. Although the bow does survive, most of the hunters use various primitive forms of muskets, if they can obtain them.

In this treeless country fuel is naturally very difficult to obtain. Its place is taken by dried dung. Outside every village will be seen large stacks of this dung, which is carefully collected by the children and placed in readiness for use. The dung burns with a very hot and more or less smokeless flame. Imported iron vessels are used for cooking. The Mongols do not usually possess any pottery, and such crocks as they have, often ware imported from a long distance, are carefully treasured. Such a condition is natural

owing to the method of their life; earthenware is too
brittle to stand the strain of continual journeys.

The houses of the Mongols, usually called by the
Mongol word yurt, are akin in type to those tents from
Northern Asia which have been described, although
the material is different.   Heavy wooden poles are
naturally extremely difficult if not impossible to obtain.
Their place is for the most part taken by a lattice
frame, although poles cannot entirely be dispensed
with.   The upright part of the tent is about a man's
height.   From this point the roof is sloped up towards
the central pole.   At the summit a space is left for
the escape of the smoke.   The framework is covered
with felt made from the wool of the flocks.   The
whole yurt is tied down firmly with ropes, which are
attached to great stones which weight the yurt and
prevent the yurt from being blown away.   Inside the
yurt will be found sheepskins, and often boxes of
Chinese manufacture.   There is a hearth in the
centre.

These tents are very rapidly dismantled.   I have
seen the women pack up their entire home in half an
hour.   The form is, it will be seen, extraordinarily
reminiscent of the tent of the Chukchee, but there are
certain important differences.   First felt has been
substituted for skins, a natural development considering the different cultural conditions of the two peoples.
Secondly, the Chukchee house is larger and more
firmly built.   In the first place it is built on the edge
of the forest where timber is more plentiful and,
secondly, where mobility is a less important factor.   I
have called attention to the fact that the Chukchee
house is, on the whole, inconveniently large for transport.   It needs as much as six sledges.   The great
size of the winter house and this comparative

immobility is perhaps partly due to the fact that the people are only just developing into a state of pastoral nomadism and have not quite adapted their belongings to these conditions.

The Mongols, on the other hand, have become acclimatized to these conditions, and have developed a house which, in spite of its unwieldy prototype, is admirably suited to steppe conditions. It is warm, it is comparatively wind-and-waterproof, and it can be easily moved. Like the Chukchee the Mongols have a second type of tent. This is not put inside the yurt, but is only used for travelling. It is a low tent, about five feet high, of the ridge pole type, usually coloured dark blue, and very light to move; it is used when they are on long journeys, and can always be seen at the various stages on the great overland routes. This type of tent is not used in the villages.

Owing to the great winds which sweep across the plains and to the scarcity of water in some places, the siting of the villages is an important factor. I am inclined to think that usually they are placed in a small subsidiary valley. Even if there is not water actually flowing in the valley bottom, and this is of comparatively rare occurrence, there is underground water, and wells dug there will normally supply the needs of the village. The small size of the subsidiary valley provides shelter which cannot be found either on the plain or in the main valley itself.

Even these villages, however, cannot be considered as more than semi-permanent; they move with the seasons and with the pasture. It is not, of course, necessary to pasture the herds in the immediate neighbourhood of the village, but they cannot be taken too far afield, both for convenience and for protection. The sheep must be pastured near the village. Another reason why the herds should be kept as close as possible to the village is the value of the droppings as fuel. The villages therefore must move from time to time; they keep more or less to the same old sites which are visited in turn according to the seasons, the excellence of a site depending so much on the wells and the consequent goodness of the pasture associated with a good supply of underground water.

The clothing of the Mongols to-day has been very much affected by the trade goods which have spread over Central Asia. Like their other possessions they are associated with the herds. The Mongol wears a long coat tied at the waist. This coat is made of sheepskin with the wool inside. He wears leather breeches and a high pointed cap, also with the wool inside. The flaps of the cap are often turned up so as to show the fleece. His boots are of the same material. They are very big and reach half-way up the calf. He seldom removes them.

Such a loose type of boot is unsuited to the use of spurs, which the Mongols do not use. They ride with a very light bit. The bridle is made of a leathern thong; they trust to their skill in horsemanship rather than to the use of bit and spur. Every pony when being ridden has a halter fastened on in addition to the bridle, and the long thong of the halter is held in the hand with the reins. The saddle is made of wood with a raised part in front and behind the rider; it is of the same type as but lighter than the Texas saddle. In spite of their skill, the Mongols are very cruel to their horses, and pay little attention to a sore back. They ride standing upright in the saddle, and shift the weight from one leg to the other. In the saddle they never seem to tire, and ride distances which to us seem incredible, keeping up with a change of ponies a distance of over a hundred miles a day. The women ride as much as the men, although they do on occasions use carts.

The ponies in use are kept tied up outside the yurts. In order to catch a pony from the herd they ride a selected fast pony who is specially trained for his speed and skill, and they catch the pony by cutting it out of the herd and lassoing it by means of a lasso which is made of a thong attached to the end of a pole. This method requires considerable speed, as it is not possible to take the pony's weight as can be done with a lasso attached to the saddle-bow; instead he must be played as a fish is played. The pony is as much a part of the Mongol as our boots are of ourselves. He is at home in the saddle literally from his earliest years, and can do little unless he is on horseback.

Trade is an important economic factor in their life, at least in the neighbourhood of the trade routes. The trade is usually in the hands not of the nomads but of the Chinese, who laugh at the simple-minded Mongols. The Mongols are, however, the camel-men, and go very great distances walking at the head of their slow-going animals, the normal distance covered by a caravan being about twenty miles a day. The journey across Gobi from Urga to Kalgan, just under 700 miles, takes about a month. In addition to riding camels some of the caravans include carts drawn by camels. The Mongols themselves trade ponies, driving down to the markets at certain places, in the old days even going as far as Peking.

I have stated earlier that the evidence suggested that the transition to agriculture from a lower stage is a direct evolution from hunting and not from pastoral nomadism. In Inner Mongolia to-day it is possible to study the change from pastoral nomadism to agriculture under particularly interesting conditions, namely, through immigration and culture-contact. The process is analogous to that which is happening in other parts of the world where the white man is displacing the other races. In the latter case, however, the change is a sudden not a gradual one.

In Inner Mongolia the boundary between the nomad and the agriculturalist, as represented by the Mongol and the Chinese respectively, has varied considerably at different times. Before the Mongols were a nation large cities were founded on the southern boundaries of Gobi, and the nomads seem to have retreated. During the Ming dynasty the nomads retreated again to the borders of Gobi, whence they had advanced under the great Khans to conquer China and to be conquered by her. When the Ming dynasty tottered to its fall in the middle of the seventeenth century the nomads again advanced as far as the great wall of China. The conquerors were Manchu Tatars, whose congeners, the various Tungusic tribes, still inhabit a large area east of Mongolia. The old cities gradually fell into ruins, and their sites became grass-grown. The advance of the nomads was so complete that even famous cities like Sindachu (Xenadu) became almost legendary.

Fifty years ago the patient Chinese agriculturalist began to advance again. He has progressed at the rate of about a mile a year, and in 1922 this was almost exactly the distance which he ploughed forward into the prairie. The effect of this advance is most striking to the observer, and seems to explain many difficulties in culture-contact and in the disappearance of races. The agriculturalist is building permanent houses. Although lean years naturally affect him, he makes use of the natural fertility of the soil to grow millet instead of wild grasses, and for the comparatively unproductive horse and sheep he substitutes the more productive ox and pig. He is therefore much less wasteful of natural resources. Under these conditions he is driving the nomads back into the northern pastures. Where the land is less fertile he passes on to the better pastures. Once he has passed the land is useless for the nomads. In some places the Mongols are learning to practise agriculture. In others, rather than abandon their old life, they are retreating.

No doubt to a certain extent this ebb and flow can be correlated with political conditions; it is also probable that it can be correlated with geographical conditions. As a final resort, however, it seems to be the conflict of two different types of economic life. In the same way that the hunter had either to give way to the nomad pastoral peoples or to the agriculturalist, so the nomad has to give way to the more productive agriculturalist. But there are certain differences in the two cases. The hunter often, though not always, either learned the new type of culture or discovered it for himself, most often no doubt the former. The pastoral nomad, however, at least in Mongolia, seems to have developed so far that he can hardly graft on to his culture other elements as I have shown the hunter may do. He therefore has perforce to retreat. In Mongolia then, we are seeing a particularly interesting type of evolution, the substitution of one race and one culture for another. To follow the arts of life of the succeeding race would be of great interest. Even, however, the Chinese agriculturalist of Chihli can by no means claim to be primitive, and he is therefore beyond the scope of this book.

America differs from the old world in having no animal which is suited for the development of pastoral nomadism, although there are plants, especially maize, which is eminently suited for cultivation. In spite of this fact, however, as Cholnoky[1] has pointed out, the beginnings of nomadic life were not unknown. Some of the Indian tribes established rights over the wild herds of buffaloes on the prairies, and allowed only a limited killing of the herds. No other tribes were permitted to hunt the herds of each tribe.

Since the introduction of domestic animals by the whites, some of the Indians have developed a very definite type of pastoral nomadism, which has taken the place of the old hunting stage. Other tribes have continued to practise the dry farming which they had learned before the advent of the invaders. These people are also of great interest because they have retained in their social organization the custom of " mother right " which has been shown to have an important part in the division of labour among those peoples who have retained it. The American tribes that I have selected as examples of desert and plain peoples are the Hopi and the Navajo, who at present inhabit reservations in Arizona.

Both these tribes live in the same country, the Navajo having a wider distribution, but their methods of life are entirely different, and it may be convenient to consider them together so that the contrast may show what different people can make of the same environment, and also how far social organization can effect inventions.

The Hopi are matripotestal. The ownership of property is mostly in the women's hands, although

[1] Cholnoky, Mem. Vol. Am. Geo. Soc. of New York, 1915, p. 142.

many of the men have their own private property. A
Hopi woman has the absolute right over her own
person. Further, in the old days when women were
captured in war they did not belong to the men who
captured them, but to the head woman of the tribe or
clan to which they actually or fictitiously belonged.
When I was stopping among the Hopi a Pima girl
was on the mesa. She had married a Hopi, and when
she had little disagreements with her husband she
went back to her " mother," i.e., the head woman of
her adopted clan. There was a case of disputed
property, and a man supported his sister's children
against his own children because the former belonged
to his clan, whereas his own children belonged to his
wife's.

Inheritance goes from mother to daughter, and the
great ambition of every Hopi woman is to possess a
kind of dower house to which her daughter can bring
her husband. Except in the case of the Mustard clan,
all the clans are exogamous. It is necessary, therefore, that a woman should buy her husband, who will
by his labour add to the property of the clan. In
certain cases a man may get property of his own by
his own labour. He will, for instance, work for wages
among the whites. At present each Hopi tries to
get sufficient dollars to buy a sewing-machine. This
belongs to him, not to his wife, and she is less anxious
to divorce him, because such a divorce means the loss
of the sewing-machine.

A divorcé or a widower is in a curious position,
because he has once been bought and therefore need
not be bought again. The presumption, I think, is
that such a man is hardly worth paying for, as he
can be worth very little. I heard of a case of a Hopi
who wished to marry a Navajo girl, a useless thing, the

Hopi matrons said, only fit to herd a few sheep in the wilderness. He had to buy her, as I shall show later in discussing Navajo customs. He paid for her partly out of the property of his own clan and partly with some animals he possessed himself. In order to make good this loss to the clan—not a very great one, as the Navajo girl, although she could not belong to her husband's clan, had to work for it—the man had to build a new clan-house, or at least help in the building.

Among the Navajo, although 'descent is in the female and not in the male line, the people have ceased to be matripotestal. No longer does the mother of the bride arrange marriages as she does among the Hopis. A man when he wishes to marry a girl arranges either personally or through his father for the price which must be paid for the girl, that is, the price of his admission to the girl's clan. It will sometimes happen that a rich old man will wish to marry a young and pretty girl. In this case the girl's people, if they happen to belong to a poor clan, will be very glad to accept the elderly lover owing to his wealth. The girl may protest sometimes successfully, but usually the marriage takes place. Among these people the men own the property.

The Hopi are essentially agriculturalists, although many of them possess horses and most are very fond of horse racing. Their principal crops are Indian corn, peaches, squashes and beans. They are skilful dry farmers. The corn is planted if possible in land where there is a certain amount of underground water. The grains are planted in holes usually about eight feet apart, although in a very dry part of the country it may be necessary to plant it even further apart. The preparation of the soil is done with digging-sticks, which are a man's most intimate possession and are usually buried on his grave upright.

The men go out in the early morning into the fields and return about ten o'clock for their breakfasts. The return is almost a ceremonial occasion, for the women in the house will give a special greeting : " We are glad that you have returned." If they fail to give this greeting a man knows that his wife will divorce him in the Hopi fashion by putting his saddle outside her door. Artificial irrigation is not practised, but the people will water the crops. When a child is ill his father will often pay special attention to the care of a particular patch of corn so that it may crop well, and then it will be used for the sick child. The cobs are gathered and put to dry on the house-roofs and then stored away in the house.

As the rain may fail, the Hopi make provision against famine, an unusual feature among primitive people, by never touching a crop till they have gathered the next one. Unless therefore they have two years famine or a succession of bad years following a failure of the crop, they do not run short. In sheltered spots, often at the foot of the mesas, they have their orchards of peaches and gardens of squashes. The latter is a favourite form of food, and is also often used as a means of bartering with the Navajo for meat. Owing to the scantiness of the vegetation the ground needs little clearing, and as they can get but small crops it does not seem to need much care.

The principal duties of the Hopi agriculturalist are to plant his crop, to water it, and to gather the corn cobs. After a time, however, owing probably to the formation of certain colloidal substances in the soil, it becomes too hard to work. The fields are then moved to spots a little further from the mesa. In some cases this process has gone on till the fields have become too distant from the mesa to be worked. The people have then had either to abandon the mesa or to starve.

It seems not improbable that this corn culture, which is the foundation of the Hopi life, comes from the south, and that in Mexico the wild grass was so improved that, by the simple method of dry farming now employed, the people manage to live. An important part in the cultivation of the soil is played by the Flute clan, who by their dances make the rain come.

On the night before the dance all the Flute people leave the village. At dawn watchers on the top of the mesa report that certain people are to be seen in the plain approaching the mesa. Messengers are sent down, and the Flute people demand admission. " What can you do? " ask the villagers. " We can bring the rain," answer the Flute people. " We have brought these to show that we can." Then they show the squashes they have brought with them, and they are admitted formally into the village on the condition that they make the crops grow. There are other dances which are concerned especially with the crops, but this one is the most picturesque and interesting. The year that I was with the Hopi the peach crop failed, a serious matter, as they had to depend for their food on the crops of the year before and the store would be less for the following year. Some of the people have sheep, but they seem to depend for the most part for their meat on the Navajo, who ride into their villages and buy squashes, giving mutton in exchange.

A few of the Navajo have fields of corn which they cultivate; for the most part, however, they depend on

the Hopi for corn. A failure of this crop will therefore affect them as much as the Hopi. The Navajo
keep large flocks of sheep. There can be little doubt
that in the old days they were hunters. The Hopi were
their enemies and they raided their mesas, probably
as much for food as for anything else. They seem to
have acquired sheep from the Spaniards, and to-day
that is their principal form of livelihood. They seem
to be able to live for long periods, if necessary, on
mutton. I have often been into a Navajo camp and
been offered a meal of meat, usually with some coffee,
the only luxury they seemed to have. The care of
the sheep devolves to a very large extent on the
children, of both sexes, for the girls as well as the
boys go out with the sheep. A Hopi man is usually
employed and kept busy by his wife. The Navajo,
now that his two principal occupations of war and
hunting are gone, has often little to do, and lets his
wife and his children do the work for him. He is,
however, usually responsible for the selling of the
meat and wool and the making of purchases.

The preparation of the food among the Hopi is a
very important business, and is in the hands of the
women. It is they who have to toil down the mesas
to the wells and to fetch the water, a very laborious
task when the mesa is six hundred feet high and the
wells perhaps two miles off. The corn is ground in
saddle-shaped querns. A stone like a rolling-pin is
used to grind the corn against the lower stone. You
will usually see three women working together. The
corn-flour is ground three times, until after the last
grinding it becomes a fine impalpable dust. This
grinding of the corn is a most important part of a
Hopi woman's life. Before she can marry she must
grind about two thousand pounds of flour; part of this

is the bridegroom's price and part the fee to the bridegroom's uncles for weaving the marriage garment and the shroud which every woman acquires when she is married.

The Hopi women are skilful potters, but the art seems to be in the hands of certain people. They do not use a potter's wheel. In making a pot they first choose a lump of clay, and putting it on a board shape it into the bottom of the pot. They then take more clay and roll it out into long sausage-shaped rolls. The potter twists this roll round the piece of clay which has been used as a foundation, and gradually builds up the pot, not by concentric rings, but in a spiral. When the pot has been entirely built up it is allowed to dry a little, and then it is carefully scraped and polished. The potters lavish a great deal of care and skill on this polishing, going over the pot again and again till it is properly shaped; they usually round off the bottom. The simpler pots are then baked and finished; the more elaborate ones have a " slip " put on them.

The clay which may be of the best consistency may not be the best for ornamental purposes; a better surface can often be obtained by pouring over the pot before it is baked a liquid solution of some other clay, very often one which turns white on baking. This extra coat of clay is known as a " slip." This white ware is often further ornamented by designs, usually of a sacred character, which are painted upon it. The pigment employed turns to a dark brown on baking.

The introduction of kerosene cans has an important effect on the potting of the villages. Although you will usually see many great big pots, often known by the Spanish name of " olla," these pots are not made any more. They are very heavy, and add considerably to the weight of the water when carrying it up to the mesa. So the women prefer to use the kerosene can. They carry it as they do the old pots, not on the head, but on the back or shoulder, taking the weight by a thong bound round the forehead. The other pots are used for the variety of household uses to which pots are put among any people. Most people seem to have a special vessel to which they are particularly attached. Together with a digging-stick a food vessel is put on the grave. No particular type seems to be used. In the graveyard you will find a great variety, including the most beautiful Hopi wares and modern cheap unbreakable china.

The Hopis also are skilful in the making of baskets. The most typical of their work are plaques, which are built up spirally like the pottery. The spiral is made up of thick twigs or collection of twigs, and these are bound together with grass fibres. They do not make the typical basketry, as our basket-makers do, in which both the warp and the weft are stiff. These baskets are often ornamented with sacred patterns, and play an important part in the ceremonial dances.

It will be seen then that the arts which are closely related to the preparation of food are highly developed among the Hopi, and that they all play an important ceremonial part. In these arts the Navajo are far less advanced. They use the saddle quern which has a wide distribution in America, but they have not brought it to such a fine art, nor can they bake the very fine, almost wafer-like cakes that the Hopi use in some of their rituals. I have never seen them using more than one grindstone, though they may do so where they have plenty of corn and therefore are more in a position to develop the technique.

They do not make or use any pottery. There are

traditions among them that at one time, in the old days, they used to make baskets and smear them with clay to make them water-tight, but I could never hear of them using true pots. To-day they buy and use iron pots whenever they can, and use them for making coffee. They have no baskets. This is all the more remarkable because baskets play an important part in their marriage ceremony. The young people sit together and partake of a meal out of the wedding-basket, and when they have so eaten they are considered to be married. These very beautiful baskets are made by Piute women. It would seem not unlikely that the Navajo must have made their own baskets at one time. The meat which they use is cooked over the fire. When they have more meat than they use they hang it in the sun to dry. They make curious store-houses. Four poles are driven into the ground, and on the top a platform is made. On this the food they have is left to dry, and the meat is suspended out of the way of the coyotes. In that dry land they have little to fear from the rain for most of the year.

The Hopi houses are for the most part very remarkable structures. The villages are built on the tops of inaccessible mesas. Some in the old days must have been exceedingly difficult to climb. The mesa top has but little space, and the houses are crowded together round a little square; they usually use the Spanish word plaza. Each house is made of dried mud and sometimes of stone. The house has normally only one room. The roof is flat, and is supported on poles. Some of these pueblo villages, for so they have been called, have brought the roof poles for their larger houses and old Spanish mission churches from very great distances. On the top of the flat roofs they dry the corn cobs. When there is not enough room in the space on top of the mesa belonging to the clan for all the houses required by the clan, another house is built on the flat roof of the one below. In some cases they have as many as three stories. The lower are usually larger in floor space, giving the upper house a kind of balcony. The approach to the top is by means of ladders, which can be drawn up in case of an attack on the village.

In addition to the built-up houses they have also underground houses, though these are only used to-day, and since a very long time, as meeting-places and for ceremonial purposes. They have been called by the Spanish name of " estufa," and by the Hopi name of kiva. In this case the entrance is from a hole in the top. A ladder extends through this hole down to the bottom of the kiva. There can be little doubt that these kivas were at one time dwellings. Some of the modern houses have holes in the roofs and a ladder so that you go down into the house as into the kiva. Such a form of dwelling had its obvious disadvantages in the case of attack. There is a Hopi tradition of the storming of Awatobi, a now uninhabited mesa. The assailants made a surprise attack and caught all the men in the kiva. They threw red peppers into the hole and burnt the incapacitated men to death.

A pueblo presents a curious appearance. It is usually perched up on the top of a high mesa. All the houses are built of adobe, and are of exactly the same colour as the earth. They seem almost like a series of termite dwellings perched one on top of the other. Usually the clans live together. In the old days, if the traditions of the population are correct, they must have been very crowded. These were the famous cities that the old Spanish adventurers,

Coronado and his companions, expected to be full of gold. There can be little wonder that they were greviously disappointed when they found them. The Hopis and the other pueblo peoples are skilful architects. They have built from such a seemingly unsatisfactory material large and interesting churches, except in the Hopi villages, where Christianity has not been accepted.

Navajo architecture is very different. Most nomad peoples have movable habitations. These peoples have never developed any form of tent, except where, as has happened to-day, they buy tents from the traders. This is probably because they have only comparatively recently acquired domestic animals. They make a very simple form of shelter in the summer out of a few cedar stems, which they roof over with leaves and desert when they move on with their flocks. They usually have two or more other houses in various parts of the country, and these they use as occasion demands. The Navajo word for house is " hogan "; I shall use it in describing their dwellings. They may be divided into various types. I shall limit myself to those which I have seen personally. In one type the walls are made by setting a series of tree-stems on end as close together as possible. The opening is usually, if not always, to the east and is broad enough for a man to go through. The walls lean rather towards the centre. On either side of the entrance short posts are set up, with a lintel over the top so as to form a door, which is closed by a sheepskin. The top is roofed over, but a central space is left through which the smoke from the fire escapes.

Some hogans are more elaborately built. The walls are made by putting logs horizontally instead of vertically, so that the hogan is polygonal in plan.

Sometimes the lower part is made of vertical logs, and the upper, from three or four feet from the ground, of horizontal logs. The height of the chimney from the ground is usually about ten feet. The more rudely constructed are covered with brushwood. These are usually used as summer hogans. The winter dwellings are smeared with mud, often the mud and brushwood are combined in a kind of rude wattle and daub. There is none of the skilled Hopi finish. When a man moves on he leaves his hogan empty. If his absence is temporary he will sometimes leave things inside, in which case he blocks up the door and the chimney. Some hogans are used for ceremonial purposes. They are often larger, but otherwise do not differ materially from the others. The sweat-houses are small hogans usually well covered with earth and often slightly sunk beneath the surface so as to conserve the heat.

The Navajo build the corrals for their flocks in much the same way as they begin to build their houses. They set a series of piles upright, so close together that the wolves and bears cannot get in. When a man dies his house is left desolate and allowed to fall into ruins. Nowadays, when they sometimes have a stone or good adobe house, they will carry the dying man outside, otherwise they would have to desert the house. There is none of the permanency of the Hopi houses.

There are no Navajo villages. Sometimes you will find a small collection of hogans which rises to the dignity of a camp or hamlet. Not infrequently the hogans are solitary or two or three together. The reason for this is not far to seek. In that arid country there is little room for many herdsmen together. The desert will feed the few flocks which support some one family group. There would not be enough pasturage for a village.

The clothing of these Indians at the moment is for the most part trade goods. It is difficult therefore for the traveller to reconstruct their old garments, even though their use has not entirely died out, and on ceremonial occasions they wear their ancient fashion, decorated of course in many special ways. Both the Hopis and the Navajo are extremely skilled in the arts of weaving. Among the former both the men and the women weave, but among the latter the industry is entirely in the hands of the women.

Apart from one or two minor differences, the textile industries of the two peoples are the same. I have often asked the Navajo what they did in the days before sheep. They have vague traditions of making a kind of cloth from vegetable fibres, but I do not think that they have any real ground for this tradition. The wool trade is for the most part confined to the Navajo, although some of the pueblo people have sheep. The wool is usually spun in a very dirty state. The wool is first carded and spun loosely into a coarse thick thread, which is wound into a ball. It is then spun a second time. The spinner kneels on her right knee and, with the right hand, rubs the spindle along her right thigh until it rotates.

The spindle they use consists of a straight piece of wood about a foot long and a third of an inch in diameter. On this, about three inches from the top, a circular disc, two inches or so in diameter, is fastened so as to enable the spinner to rotate the spindle. She holds up the spindle by a piece of thread that has already been spun, and the twisting movement is imparted to the unspun thread so that it becomes tightly twisted. The spinner pulls out the thread with the left hand, continually stopping to remove impurities. As soon as she has spun a little she winds it round the spindle. Such a process is considerably assisted if a little hook is fastened at the top of the spindle, but the Navajo do not use such a hook. The thread is usually spun three times in order to ensure that the threads are even and sufficiently twisted.

The loom on which the blankets are woven is usually a big but simple structure outside the house. Two beams sometimes as much as ten feet high are set upright. They are so cut that there may be a fork at the top. In the fork a cross-bar is laid, and from this a beam is suspended to which the warp is fixed. The weaver separates the threads with her fingers, and often weaves most elaborate patterns. They also use a small horizontal loom, kept taut by a band round the weaver's back, the other end being fastened to a post, wall or tree. These small looms are only used for weaving narrow fabrics for belts and so on.

It will be seen that this culture is peculiarly suited to special conditions. The evolution of this culture is in some respects very recent, and it is therefore of particular interest, showing as it does how a people who in many respects are very primitive can adopt certain features which are imported by an alien culture, and can incorporate them into a culture of their own.

CHAPTER XIII

LABOUR IN TROPICAL FORESTS

THE dwellers in tropical forests have always exercised a peculiar fascination over the mind of civilized man, because among them the picture of our remote ancestors seemed again to be reproduced. Here under the shadow of the giant trees various primitive races of hunters are still to be found, and it is by no means impossible that it was under such conditions that man originally developed. The most primitive skull that has hitherto been found comes from Java, and all the apes which survive are tropical forest-dwellers. Such primitive forest-dwellers are to be found in the equatorial forests of the old and the new world. The examples which I have chosen for special study live in the Malay Peninsula. They have been studied very carefully by Skeat and Blagden, and to their book I am especially indebted for much which follows.

The overpowering nature of the environment cannot but strike the observer. All or most of the animals which live in these forests are specially adapted for forest life, unlike many of the dwellers in temperate forests. The plants show a still greater adaptation. Man also has been profoundly modified by the conditions of an environment which may have been his original home. " The shadow, the hall-mark of the primeval forest—at once their protector, their sustainer, and their grave—is burned into them, and shows itself in the restless motion and hunted expression of their eyes, and even in their very gait, for the great height to which they raise the foot in walking (a habit acquired in circumventing the continual obstacles that meet them in the undergrowth), and the careful deliberation with which they plant it on the ground, remain even when they come out into the open country, and expose them to much ridicule and cheap witticisms on the part of Malays."

" It was the forest which supplied them with food, shelter, clothing, ornaments, implements of every description. . . . It was the forest that received their dead into its kindly bosom; indeed, to be laid to rest in the cool outstretched arms of the great forest trees was the highest honour that could be paid to their departed chiefs." [1]   In discussing the relation of the man to his environment Skeat draws especial attention to the way in which man adapts himself by means of mechanical devices. This important aspect of man's arts of life is abundantly brought out by the examples which they have collected of the mode of life in the forests of the Malay Peninsula.

Before discussing the arts of life of these tribes it is necessary to point out that their arts of life depend on many other things besides a mere mechanical adaptation to these very devastating surroundings. With all the mechanical devices of civilization at his disposal the white man has not been able sufficiently to adapt himself to that environment so as to live there permanently. The adaptation of the primitive tribes is, however, not a mere mechanical adaptation. The

[1] Skeat and Blagden, " The Pagan Races of the Malay Peninsula," p. 13.

physiological needs of the tropics are very different from those of the other extreme of climate, the Arctic, and the discussion of the arts of life will show not only a difference of technique due to different raw materials, but also a fundamental difference in many arts due to the different demands of the body which the tropics make.

In the north the climate needs the expenditure of a great deal of energy to keep the body mechanism working. The tropics, while demanding protection from heat and light, require less energy to keep alive. The north seems to cause a perpetual craving for rich flesh food to keep up the bodily heat; the refreshing power of fruits are more welcome in the tropics. Natural resources are also, of course, very different. While most of the very primitive peoples in the north are dependent mainly on hunting for their food, the forest-dwellers of the tropics prefer a greater amount of fruits and vegetables.

The same characters which have made for the development of fur-bearing animals have also made for the value of their skins to man living on the northern borders of cold forests. In the tropics such a covering is hardly needed to sustain life. Clothing, therefore, certainly an art of life in the north, is rather concerned with the decorative arts in the tropical forests.

The seasonal character of the climate in the north contrasts very strongly with its comparatively unvarying nature in the tropics, and so again alters the arts of life. Thrift, a necessity where the winters are long and cold, though not always practised, is unnecessary in a forest where the seasonal changes are confined to a difference in humidity. To eat putrescent animals is feasible in the north; it is unthinkable in the tropics where the processes of decay are so rapid.

To eat cold dried fish uncooked is possible in Hokkaido, but in Java, though fish form an important element in diet, they must be cooked soon after death if they are to be eaten at all.

The races of the Malay Peninsula, other than the civilized Malays, Indians and Chinese, may be conveniently divided into three groups—Semang, Sakai, and Jakun. All these peoples are primitive, although in slightly differing degrees; they differ considerably in physique, and a comparison of their differing cultures is therefore particularly instructive for our present purpose.

The Semang are the most nomadic of all the tribes. They have woolly hair and dark skins, and belong to the negrito physical type, which is also found in the Philippine and in the Andaman Islands. The Sakai are still for the most part nomadic, but belong to a very different physical type. They are much lighter in colour; they have curly hair and long narrow heads. They belong possibly to the same stock as the Veddas of Ceylon. The third group, Jakun, are straight-haired with smooth blue-black hair. They may be conveniently called savage Malays.

The staple food of all the nomadic tribes are wild vegetables, including yams, roots and the numerous fruits which grow in the forest. When these supplies are insufficient they make up their diet by fishing, hunting and trapping. The tribes who are a little more advanced have learned the value of rice, and barter it for an extravagant rate from the Malays.

The method of agriculture of the most primitive tribes consists simply in throwing away the seeds of the fruits which they have eaten. Fruit seeds or seedlings are planted among the first crops that are raised. In spite of the fact that rice forms the most important article of diet among the Malays, the wilder tribes have not discovered methods of growing it. They usually apparently begin their agriculture by planting millet in a clearing; this stage is followed by that in which they barter rice and possibly begin to grow a kind of half-wild hill rice as opposed to the irrigated rice of the valleys.

This final stage is accompanied by the cultivation of bananas, tapioca, maize and sweet potatoes. Owing to the fact that they only know the hill rice, they cultivate a fresh plot every year. This final stage is only reached by the most advanced tribes; it represents not a case of evolution but of culture-contact. The first crop grown is not indigenous, but is probably a kind of Chinese millet. We have then a good example of a tribe progressing owing to alien influence. Their agriculture is practised with the aid of much magic, which may be said to constitute probably the most important part of their agricultural processes.

Most of the wild tribes, like all primitive peoples, are very adept in tracking wild animals, even though the pursuit of them is only a final resort when other food fails. The Sakai use a blow-pipe, the Semang a bow. The tribes also possess a rude kind of adze and a jungle knife, which is made of a sharp sliver of bamboo. The tribes who have come much into contact with the Malays have iron-pointed spears, but the others use spears made out of bamboos or palm. The Jakun and the Malays use throwing-sticks. Hatchets are obtained by barter or copied from the Malays. All the tribes are now in possession of fire-arms, usually old-fashioned " Tower muskets."

The game hunted is very various. It includes occasionally even such large animals as the tiger and the elephant, both of which are hunted and eaten.

Practically all the wild animals are utilized by the various tribes, though their use depends partly on the district and partly on the food-supplies available at the time. They avoid the toad, the scorpion and some snakes and insects, but otherwise, among the bigger mammals, they hunt deer and wild pig and various species of monkeys, and among smaller mammals squirrels, porcupines, flying-foxes and rats. Birds, including argus pheasants, peacocks, herons and hornbills, and reptiles such as tortoises, lizards and snakes, all contribute to the meals of these primitive peoples.

The Sakai fish with weirs, a practice that they have probably learnt from the Malays, with rod and line, with nets, and by poisoning the streams. The wilder of the Semang tribes live far up in the mountains where few fish are available, but those tribes which live near the rivers make great use of fish; usually it is eaten fresh, but it would appear that sometimes it is dried. The smaller fish and fry are caught in shallows and pools by means of a basket made of bamboo in the form of a scoop. This method has naturally a limited application, and most of the fishing is done with a rod and line.

The rod is a straight unpeeled stick about six feet long, to the end of which a line of twisted strands of bark of a slightly longer length is fastened. The Malays know the use of the reel, but the negritoes seem unacquainted with its use. Hooks are made of brass or other wire. Quite large fish and tortoises are captured with fish spears and harpoons. Among the tribes at Siong the latter implement is made of the leaf-stem of a large palm, and is about ten feet long.

Some of the Jakun, Besisi, are expert fishermen with the rod and line. They use mud-worms as bait, and most of the fishing is done by the women. They have one unusual method, which is also practised by the Malays. At about half tide they row in one of the numerous mangrove creeks which everywhere line the shore. At suitable spots they beat the water with the point of their rod, which is only about two feet long with a three foot line. The splashing attracts mud-fish, who greedily swallow the bait.

The division of labour in all these varied occupations is on the general lines which we find elsewhere. The heavier work of fighting and of hunting is done by the men, who also do the trapping; the women fish and collect roots and fruits. The women also do the cooking, though their most important industry is the making of baskets.

The Semang and the Sakai have similar methods of cooking, but the Jakun have learned other ways of preparing their food. Among the wilder tribes sometimes the flesh is eaten absolutely raw, although usually the flesh is slightly roasted. The meat is inserted in a cleft-stick, which is inclined at an angle over the fire. Fish is treated in the same way. Yams and roots are grated and then wrapped up with long sections of banana leaf, and are then baked. Their method of cooking rice, when they possess it, is to dry it before the fire in a green internode of bamboo. These vessels are carried about, and when the people want rice they break them open. A few of the inland peoples and the primitive Malays who live along the coast have acquired by barter from the more civilized Malays the ordinary Malay rice pots and other kitchen gear.

These primitive peoples provide in their dwellings a very good example of the gradual evolution of human habitations, and also show a close parallelism with some of the earliest inhabitants of Europe. The Semang are truly nomads; they have no permanent homes, and the wilder ones at least do not stop for more than three days in one place. The evolution of the various types of habitations is thus traced by Skeat and Blagden. The most primitive form is the rock shelter which is commonly used. They seem, on the whole, to avoid caves and to prefer the true rock shelter of an over-hanging ledge. The next stage is stated by these authors to be a tree shelter. In its simplest form a screen of leaves is fixed across the branches of a tree a little above the fork to serve as a kind of roof. This finally develops into the true tree-hut.

It is suggested that possibly this form of dwelling developed as protection against elephants. That it represents a stage in development seems for some reasons unlikely, because the anthropoid apes make use of an arboreal hut of this kind. As a protection against elephants it is extremely probable, as a simple hut of this kind is certainly used for this purpose in Ceylon among the more primitive peoples.

The palm leaf ground screen in many of its features seems to be a direct descendant of the cave shelter, recalling it as it does so closely. It is made of three or four stout sticks, which are driven into the ground at an angle. They are covered with palm leaves which are so fastened that the rain cannot penetrate. From this simple form of shelter the true hut is evolved.

They make a kind of hemispherical shelter which is frequently known as a " bee-hive hut." From this the communal shelter is an easy and probable develop-ment, if indeed the two did not evolve side by side. A true hut was possibly first of all used as a store before it became a home for man. The Sakai have shelters and tree huts and also true huts, but these latter are rectangular and not round as among the negritoes.

The sea people often live not in huts on land but on sampans in the creeks. Such people are to be found to-day in many varying stages of culture along the shores of South-Eastern Asia. They were the only inhabitants of Singapore when it was first visited by Sir Stamford Raffles, who decided to make it into a great merchant depot. Although there is thus a great variety in the types of houses among the aboriginal tribes of the Malay Peninsula, we may generalize and say that the negritoes prefer either tree shelters, except perhaps some of the wilder ones, or huts on the ground. The other tribes prefer to build their huts on piles to using either tree shelters or any other form of house.

Their clothing is always of the simplest form. They do not wear skins or feathers. Their usual article of dress is a girdle made out of the long rhizomorph of some fungus or a fringe of leaves. Sometimes coiled cane and bark is worn. Bark cloth is also made and used. Bands are worn on the upper part of the arm, the wrist and just below the knee. These primitive garments are, however, rapidly going out of use, and the ordinary Malay dress with a sarong jacket and handkerchief is being substituted. It is worthy of remark that often underneath this newly acquired finery the old and simple girdle is worn.

I have alluded in many places to the influence which the Malays have upon the tribesmen. The presence of the latter in these remote regions is almost entirely due to trade. In the old days this seems to have been of the silent variety, to-day the trading is usually done through an intermediary less timid than the rest. It is said that the Malays fleece the aborigines unmercifully, and that the latter much prefer to deal with the

Chinese traders. They purchase implements, tools and weapons, cooking utensils and cloth, and some of the minor luxuries of civilization, such as mirrors and ornaments. They also obtain rice, the value of which they have learned from the Malays, tobacco, salt and areca nuts. In return the Malays obtain from them the varied produce of the jungle—perfumed woods, oils, gutta and dammar. The aborigines also procure small quantities of tin.

Although the Veddas of Ceylon have been much changed and have lost many of their primitive characters owing to contact with the more advanced Cingalese, they present a very interesting comparison with the tribes we have just been studying, possessing as they do some more advanced and some more primitive features. Their social relationships have more recently been studied by Dr. Seligman, and the whole of the available literature together with many original observations have been published by the brothers Sarasin.

The Vedda community is very primitive in its organization. Each family is made up of the parents and unmarried children and usually the married daughters and their husbands. Usually a single family or small groups of two families live and hunt together. Ascending in the scale there is normally a community which consists of from one to five families who, although they do not hunt together, share the rights of hunting over a bit of land and of gathering honey and fishing and also of using the rock shelters.[1]

The staple food of these people is flesh, although there enters into their diet a considerable admixture of vegetable foods. Sarasin considers that flesh is a recent development from an original vegetarian diet.

[1] Seligman, " The Veddas," p. 62.

The most important of their food animals is the deer, but numerous other mammals are eaten. Fish forms an important part of their diet. Yam is the staple vegetable food and bread-fruit is the principal fruit eaten. They also eat the leaves of many plants and even the bark, especially the cambium of the wild mango. Fallen wood is consumed mixed with honey. It is possible that this is only used in time of need, but more probably the indigestible cellulose forms a convenient medium whereby they can make better physiological use of the honey, as agar-agar is sometimes used by physicians. Honey in any case is always an important article in their diet. They seem sometimes to obtain rice by barter and also such narcotics as tobacco and betel. They do not appear to use salt and they drink water.

Their most important weapon for hunting is the bow. This, when unstrung, measures about six feet in length. They make a bowstring of bast about three centimetres broad, twisted spirally. The arrows usually have a wooden shaft and are tipped with iron, which they obtain by barter. The bow is feathered by having feathers bound to it. They also possess in the axe a universal weapon both for defence and also for cutting down trees and other labours. The bow is used to shoot both animals and fish. Their only domestic animal, the dog, is used for hunting small animals like hares and also as a watch-dog. In this connexion it is of interest to note that the Punans of Borneo, who in many ways resemble the Veddas in their modes of life, do not possess dogs and do all their hunting by themselves.

Their other tool apart from the bow and the axe is the digging-stick, which plays, as it does among the Bushmen, a very important part in their culture. It

is usually about the height of a person, and used chiefly
by the women for digging yams. The roots are cut
and are replaced in the earth, a practice which also
occurs among the Australians. It is possible that in
this very primitive operation we may see the beginning
of the primitive type of " hackbau " agriculture.

Some of the tribes have learned the use of a primitive
type of pottery, but this is in all probability a recent
acquisition. Normally they roast their meat and fish.
Sometimes the former is dried till it is board-hard and
tasteless, in any case it is never eaten raw. It is
always mixed to a greater or lesser extent with honey.
The yam is eaten apparently more by the women than
the men, as frequently happens the women seem to
prefer, or at any rate habitually use, more vegetarian
food than the men. The yams are put into the fire
until they are charred black.

Contact with other races has considerably affected
the Vedda form of habitation. There can be little
doubt, however, that the Veddas originally lived, as
some of them do to-day, in rock shelters. They seemed
not to have built huts, although it is very possible
that they did take refuge in the higher branches of
big trees out of the way of elephants. The rock
shelters are in no sense caves, but rather a place
where owing to the erosion of water or other agencies
space has been left under an overhanging ledge of
rock. This provides shelter from the weather,
especially necessary where the rainfall is heavy.
These shelters are inhabited from time to time and
abandoned when owing to their insanitary nature they
become uninhabitable. This type of dwelling is of
particular interest because it coincides closely with the
type of home used by the early inhabitants of Europe.
Where these ledges are not available the Veddas

construct shelters out of leaves supported on poles, a type of habitation that strongly recalls the rock shelter which has no doubt served as a model.

Their clothing is of the simplest description, and consists of a piece of bark-cloth, which is worn as a bandage round the loins by the men and as a short skirt by the women. Contact with the more civilized Cingalese has affected their primitive methods of trading, but some of the older travellers report that they were in the habit of practising the silent trade.

In the forests of Borneo there survive nomad hunters who in some ways are as primitive or even more primitive than the Veddas. These people, the Punans, have been carefully described by Hose and McDougall.[1] They live in a small community of twenty to thirty adults and about the same number of children. They have a chief, although he possesses little more authority than that which naturally falls to a man who is of considerable age and experience. The property of each individual is closely merged in the group, and all share any food that any member may have obtained. It is usual for a man when he returns home after successful hunting to throw down the game in the centre, and it is not considered to belong to the hunter.

Unlike the Veddas, the Punans have no domestic animals, not even dogs, which are possessed by most primitive peoples. They live entirely on wild products. The most important of the vegetable jungle produce is vegetable tallow, which is found in the seed of *Shorea* and wild sago. They eat practically any type of animal which they can catch, and being daring hunters will even kill the rhinoceros. The game is usually killed with poisoned darts from the blow-pipe. The universal use of this weapon is of interest,

---

[1] " Pagan Tribes of Borneo."

because it is made not with the tools which the people themselves can make out of jungle produce but with a rod made of imported iron. It is impossible to say how the Punans hunted before they had access to iron.

Their other tools and weapons also include things which belong to an alien culture. In addition to the blow-pipe with a spear blade attached, every Punan carries with him, when he goes away from his home, a small axe with a long narrow blade which he uses for working camphor out of the heart of the camphor tree, a small knife and a sword.

Their domestic utensils are, as might be expected, more primitive. They do possess a few iron pots; formerly, and still on occasions, they used green bamboo as a cooking vessel. They have tongs of bamboo, and the rest of their possessions are made of hardwood, and include sago-mallets and sieves, dishes, spoons and spatulas. Sago is still sometimes boiled in the cups of the pitcher plant. These few things, together with a few mats of plaited rattan and some small bamboo boxes, constitute all their possessions.

A few of the Punans live in limestone caves, possibly the survival of what was usual in the old days. Most, however, live in a kind of low shelter which is crudely made of palm leaves. This shelter is supported on sticks so as to form a sloping roof. Three sides are open, and the rain can beat freely through the leaves. They wear a loin-cloth of bark and beads round the wrist or ankles, or both, and sometimes below the knees. Unlike their more advanced neighbours, they never build boats and are never happy unless they are in the shadow of the forest.

Apart from the fact that they have learned the use of iron these forest-dwellers are almost as primitive as any type of man which yet survives. It is more than probable that they used stone tools in the old days, which of course will survive. Unless we had accounts of their present state of culture it would be impossible to reconstruct their manner of life. The iron soon rusts if exposed to equatorial rains. The rest of their possessions are rapidly swallowed up in the jungle. If they became extinct or changed their manner of life it would be impossible to trace them, and all that the searching archæologist would find, if he were lucky, would be a few scattered human bones.

CHAPTER XIV

LABOUR IN THE FOREST CLEARINGS

IN the previous pages I have been dealing with peoples, most of them in an extremely ill-developed state of culture, who depend mainly if not entirely on the products of the jungle for their daily bread. In most parts of Asia those tribes and nations who live in the true tropical savanna or meadow-land are in a very advanced state of culture and therefore beyond the scope of this book. In Borneo, however, we find numerous peoples who depend chiefly on rice for their nutrition and therefore resemble the great majority of the peoples of South-Eastern Asia, but who at the same time have by no means separated themselves entirely from the jungle. They have not learned yet to manure their rice-fields, and therefore they are compelled to cut down the virgin forest to make new fields at frequent intervals. It must be remembered that here the vegetation is very luxuriant, and it has been estimated that after cultivation the forest is entirely restored and in all appearance virgin within the space of two hundred and fifty or three hundred years.

We are perhaps hardly justified therefore in calling this culture a true savanna culture. I have, however, noticed it because we can see here in its most primitive form the rice culture which extends from the Dutch

Indies to far-away Japan, and which has given rise to a type of agriculture which feeds a great part of the human race.

In Europe it is difficult except by archæological methods to follow all the steps in the evolution of the forest-meadow culture from which our civilization took its rise. In Asia we are more fortunate in that we can trace from the primitive jungle dweller the gradual evolution of a meadow culture, different in that it is a warm meadow and not a cold meadow, from the early forest culture. All exist side by side. The jungle man I have discussed; the early meadow man forms the subject of this chapter.

Thence we could follow by easy stages the gradual rise of that culture which has filled the valleys of the Hwang Ho and the Yangtse Kiang with little rice-field after rice-field, and has produced a culture which two hundred years ago was little if at all inferior to our own.

This primitive rice culture in Borneo has been dealt with very exhaustively by Hose and McDougall in their book on the "Pagan Races of Borneo," and this book forms the principal authority for the pages which follow. All the people living in the interior of this island, except for some primitive peoples as, for instance, the Punans and the Malanans, consider rice to be the principal foodstuff except for a few weeks in the year, at which time the jungle fruits are most abundant and then form the principal article of diet. At all other times rice is used at breakfast, dinner and supper, and forms the greater part of all those meals.

Tapioca, maize, sweet potatoes, pumpkins, bananas, cucumbers, millet, pine-apples, chillies, are grown regularly but only as a secondary crop. They and wild sago are used to make up a deficiency in rice in times of scarcity, but they are always considered as a poor substitute. Rice-eating peoples in Eastern Asia have told me that although it is possible for them to live on a continued diet of rice they have found that they cannot live on sweet potatoes, and that therefore they only grow a few of them.

The fields in Borneo are closely surrounded by the forest, and therefore their agriculture is continually threatened by numerous enemies. Their methods are extremely simple. The Dusuns and some of the Murut people in North Borneo have learnt the use of the plough probably from the Chinese colonists, many of whom in this area, in contradistinction to the Chinese in Java for instance, are agriculturalists. Elsewhere the plough is unknown. A few peoples have acquired a knowledge of the practice which prevails in the Philippines and in other parts of Indonesia, of walking a water-buffalo up and down the fields while they are flooded before the seed is sown, a practice that foreshadows the use of the buffalo with the plough. Elsewhere this practice is as yet unknown. The Kelabits know the elementary principles of irrigation and turn water on to their fields from the streams.

Apart from these examples the rice growing is as simple as possible. Each family has a patch, usually of about four acres, which corresponds to the size which the strength of the family, including the slaves, can work. The site selected is if possible near a river, so that easy access can be gained by boat. Where the patch is in the jungle they build corduroy paths to it. The patch is also on the hillside. The slope makes the felling of timber much easier, and also secures better drainage.

When an area has been selected the men of the family begin by clearing the undergrowth, and then with the

assistance of their neighbours proceed to fell the trees.
Platforms are erected sufficiently high up the bole to
avoid the buttressed base so characteristic of the great
forest trees. They then cut into the bole with their
two-handed axes, but without felling the trees. All
the big trees in the area selected are thus cut. The
field to be cleared is roughly triangular in shape with
the apex pointing uphill and the base on the river,
the reason for this will appear shortly.

When the cutting of the trees is complete, they fell
one or two at the top of the field. They are directed
very carefully, and in their fall bring down all the
small timber and start an avalanche which includes
all the big trees which have been cut already. The
wrecked forest is then allowed to dry, a process which
takes about a month if the weather is dry. During
the time of waiting the men spend the time in sowing
some of the lesser crops, a little early rice, some
maize, sweet potatoes and tapioca. At this time also
the agricultural implements are repaired and set in
order. When the timber is dry it is burned, and as
soon as the ashes are cool the sowing begins. After a
crop is harvested a field is allowed to lie fallow for
two years. The rank growth is then burnt off again.
This is done three or four times, and then the field
is abandoned.

It is said that after ten years it can be used again,
but even then the crop is comparatively poor, and
each year a new piece of virgin forest is added. In
spite of the immense labour that these primitive
methods entail the people therefore find it continually
necessary to cut down the forest. The immense
populations that such rice-growing areas as Java
possess are therefore quite impossible, and, although
the people are no longer nomadic, it is necessary to

move their villages at comparatively short intervals in order to continue to find fertile fields.

During the sowing the men and women work together. The men go in front making holes with pointed sticks about six inches apart. The women follow, each with a seed-basket round her neck. They throw three or four seeds into each hole but do not cover them up. The whole process takes up the whole of the dry season, which only lasts about two months. The grain grows very rapidly when the rains come, and is well above the ground after a few days. All the sowing of a field is not done at the same time, as they wish the whole crop to ripen at the same time. Different kinds of rice are grown in different parts of a clearing, and most of the different sorts take a slightly different time to ripen, which varies from about fourteen to twenty weeks.

Huts are built in the padi fields during this period so that the owners can guard the crops against their many enemies. First they make contrivances of bamboos and rattans to scare away the birds. The plot is then fenced to keep out the wild deer and pig. When this fence has been built the men have finished their share of agriculture till the harvest, and go on long excursions into the jungle to gather wild produce or pay visits or engage in war.

The care of the fields devolves on the women. They weed each patch at least twice at intervals of about a month. They use a hoe which looks like a flattened hook at the end of a short handle. The work is very carefully and laboriously done, and is very fatiguing; the woman stoops as she works and hoes out all the weeds round each plant, a process which needs about three weeks if all the clearing is to be hoed. When they are not hoeing the early crops are harvested, and at this time they will spend several weeks on the clearing, using the temporary hut at night. The growth of the crop is watched by everybody with the very greatest interest, and as soon as the ears are formed but are not yet ripe some are gathered, the heads are beaten flat and they are dried in the sun, but not cooked, and are eaten.

The harvest is a very important period, and all—men women and children—take part. The crop at this time is attacked by many birds in spite of the scare devices. The people therefore walk through the fields and gather those ears which are ripe. The knife which they use has a wide distribution, even among those rice-eating peoples whose methods of agriculture is much more advanced. It consists of a piece of wood into which a small blade is inserted along one side. A piece of bamboo is inserted in the side opposite to that in which the blade is fastened. This bamboo stands out perpendicularly to the axis of the blade. The knife is held in the hand, the bamboo preventing it from slipping. The harvester grasps the bottom of the ears with the thumb and presses it against the blade. The ear is held in the fingers and put into a basket which is suspended round the neck.

This method of gathering rice, crude and simple as it appears, is practised very widely among much more advanced peoples. Although the knife used is very different, it is a method of reaping that is distributed among many agriculturalists; dhurra, for instance, in the Sudan, is gathered by a closely analogous process. The straw is not used.

The ears are dried on platforms outside the house. They are placed on coarse mats, under which one with a finer mesh has been placed. The ears are stamped with the bare feet and the grain falls through on to the finer mat. The grain is again dried in the sun and is then carried with much merry-making to the family barns. The harvest festival begins with the selection of the seed corn by certain skilled old women. The seed-baskets are never quite emptied, but are always allowed to retain a little of the old seed from the year before so that there may be continuity of crop. When this has been done the carnival of the year begins.

This selection of the seed by the women is of great interest, and seems to recall the earlier periods in history which I have paralleled among many peoples where the collecting of the wild seeds is in the hands of the women or the whole of the agriculture is done by them.

The people spend so much time on the rivers that it is natural that they have become skilful fishermen. They use most commonly the cast net. Their nets when wide open may have an area as big as a circle six feet in diameter. A strong cord is tied to the centre of the net, which is cone-shaped. The edge is weighted with stones or sinkers of metal. They use this type of net in both deep and shallow water. In the former case at least two men are needed; one manages the canoe, the other stands at the bows with the cord in his right hand. He first throws a stone to imitate a fruit falling in the water, and when the fish rush to the spot he casts his net. If the fish are small they become entangled in the meshes of the net. If a large fish has been caught a man dives overboard and secures the open part of the net.

Sometimes this seine net is used at the mouths of small tributary streams, in which case the fish are driven down towards it. Sometimes flat nets are stretched across a stream. The women use a net which is shaped like our prawning net, which, of course, can only be used in shallow pools. In addition to these nets, whose use is simple, they have several ingenious forms of nets. The most usual is a square net which is stretched out and kept below water. The end of the framework which keeps the net outstretched is fastened to some form of lever so that the net can be raised rapidly. In some cases a bait or lure is placed above the net. When a fish swims over the net the fisherman pulls the lever and the net is rapidly raised and the fish caught. Angling is also commonly practised. A kind of crude spoon bait is sometimes used. The Kayan make hooks out of brass wire with a single barb. The Kenyas take their fish with a double barbed hook made out of a piece of rattan with the thorns which the plant uses for climbing still attached.

The fish-traps in use, although they vary in detail, correspond in principle to our lobster pots. They make a double cone out of bamboo. The large cone has an open mouth but closed apex. The smaller cone is fastened into the larger cone so as to block the mouth. The apex is made of springy bamboo slips which open readily outwards. The trap is set with the apex pointing up-stream. The fish enters the mouth of the cone and passes readily through the bamboos, which give. Once it has passed into the larger cone it cannot get out again. A simpler form of this trap is a single cone of bamboo in which the fish get wedged and cannot extricate themselves. All these devices are further elaborated; the people have a kind of baited lobster pot for prawns, and a large trap, the entrance to which is effected by a door with a valve similar to the double cone.

The largest scale, however, on which fish are caught

is by poisoning the water with the juice of a plant. This plant is grown in little patches on the rice-fields. They gather a large quantity and build a fence across the stream into which they let traps. All the boats are taken out and are partially filled with water. The plants are beaten so that all the juice is extracted and runs into the water at the bottom of the boats. At a signal all this is thrown into the water either by baling or by upsetting the boats. The boats are then got ready, and after a time the fish appear stupefied at the top of the water; they are caught by being clubbed or with nets. In the shallow streams tickling is practised. Crocodiles are not normally hunted for food but only to revenge somebody who has been killed by one of these beasts. Elaborate precautions are in any case taken so that no one shall have to bear the onus of having killed a crocodile.

Pigs are usually hunted by a party of several men with a small pack of about five dogs. The dogs chase the pig until it turns on them, and hold it at bay till the men arrive and kill it with their spears, a method not without danger both to the men and dogs. During the season when the wild fruit is ripe the pigs sometimes migrate and swim rivers. The men will at times intercept them during their passage and kill them from boats. The Kenyas and Klemantans catch deer by driving them into a corral which is made of a rope of rattan to which nooses are attached. Most of the animals get caught in the nooses and are speared. The blow-pipe is used to kill birds and monkeys, and sometimes even pig and deer, especially by the wilder tribes.

Their traps are numerous. A gap is made in the fence round the padi field in order to catch pig and deer. Beside the gap a bamboo spear is fastened with the butt lashed to a springy green pole. The spring is bent back and fastened with rattan attached to a trigger. The animal in its attempt to pass through the gap releases the trigger and the spear is driven forcibly across the gap into it. Sometimes the spring is set vertically. For small animals they use a spring which catches the animal in a noose and holds it dangling. The Argus pheasant is caught by putting sharp splinters of bamboo in its dancing places. The birds as they endeavour to clear the dancing place wound themselves and, loosing much blood, fall an easy victim to the hunter. The ground pigeon is caught by imitating its notes on a whistle till it comes near enough to be snared.

In addition to hunting, the wild products of the jungle are also collected. Besides fruits, these include gutta, rubber, camphor, rattans, beeswax, honey, vegetable tallow, wild sago, dammar and edible birds' nests. The men go out in small parties, and may be absent for as much as weeks at a time. They pull their boat under the undergrowth and conceal it there, and while in the jungle live in rude shelters. Wild sago is abundant and is much used when there is a shortage of rice. The people also hunt monkeys and porcupines for bezoar stones, which are much used by the Chinese for medicine. The stones are found in the animals' kidneys or gall-bladder. The most important jungle produce is, however, edible birds' nests. There are several varieties, but all are to be found on the roofs and the walls of caves, the white nests in low caves and the black in very lofty ones. The caves are the property of an individual and are inherited. In order to gather the nests a lofty bamboo scaffolding has in some cases to be erected.

The methods of preparing food are more elaborate

than those which we have been considering previously. The water vessels that they use are made of bamboo. It would seem that in the old days they did make a kind of crude pottery, but its use has been entirely superseded by imported Chinese ware. They now cook their rice in a kettle made of iron or brass shaped "like an old English cauldron." This is either suspended over the fire or else is supported on a tripod which is made of stones. A few plates have been obtained from the traders, but a leaf usually serves as a platter. They make dishes and plates also out of hardwood. Vegetables and fish are cooked in a kind of open stew-pan.

The ordinary day's routine, in relation especially to the work of the women in preparing the food, is described very vividly by Hose and McDougall. The women rise before dawn and boil the rice for breakfast and for the dinner of those who are going to be away all day. They then feed the pigs and afterwards settle down to their various tasks. A few men remain in the house, making boats, forging swords, axes, spear-heads or hoes, or mending those which have been broken. Others go out to hunt or fish or to gather jungle produce.

During December and January everything is neglected in favour of the gathering of wild fruits, on which they practically live at this time of year. Except then and during the rice season the women are employed entirely about the house. The greater part of their work consists of the preparation of rice. The rice is put out to dry in the morning, then they get dinner, which consists of boiled rice with fish, pork or fowl, and is eaten as are all the meals in the private rooms which will be described later. After dinner they pound rice.

The mortar consists of a log with a large hole hollowed out in it. The rice is poured into this and two women work together. Each holds a pestle, a long heavy stick, and pounds the rice alternately, sweeping back into the mortar the rice which is spilled in the pounding. The monotonous beat of the padi pounders, especially when heard through the dense foliage which so often surrounds a village in the islands, is a most characteristic sound. The work is very heavy, and is often undertaken entirely by the younger women, who hand over the winnowing to the older ones. Winnowing is done with a mat which is shaped like a dustpan. The grain is then sifted and ready for use. The refuse forms the principal food of the pigs. The work is a dusty one, and when it is finished the women go and bathe in the river and then get supper, for by this time everybody is coming home from the jungle.

The Punans are nomadic forest-dwellers, but otherwise all the other pagan peoples of Borneo build a similar type of house, although there are differences in the size and the proportions. The best built ones are those of the Kayans, and serve as a good type. A house of average dimensions will hold forty to fifty families, which with slaves will give it a population of from two to three hundred. A larger one may hold twice as many. A house is always built close to the river, usually not more than fifty yards away and parallel to the course of the stream. The plan is that of a long and narrow rectangle. The roof is a simple ridge which extends the whole length of the house. It is covered with shingle made of hardwood. The framework of the roof is carried by massive iron-wood piles at a height of about twenty-five feet from the ground. Rather over the height of a man from the cross-beams of the roof the same piles hold the floor, of which the cross-beams are mortised on to the piles. Over these cross-beams enormous planks are laid parallel to the long axis of the house. The projecting eaves are prolonged to a height of about four or five feet from the floor. This space is left open, and gives light and air to the house and allows a free view of the river. It is quite open except for a low parapet which is made at the outer edge of the floor.

The floor space is about two hundred yards long and thirty to sixty yards broad. Vertical planks are set upright a little to the river side of the middle line, and divide the house into two parts. The river side is undivided and forms a continuous gallery, but the other part is divided up at intervals of thirty feet or a little less in a series of large rooms. Each of these rooms belongs to a family, and forms the sleeping-room of the father, mother, daughters, young sons and female slaves. It contains small alcoves for sleeping chambers and a fireplace. It is also used for the family meals.

There are fireplaces at intervals along the great gallery, and along the inner side the villagers put the things which are in constant use—the rice mortars, the winnowing mats, paddles, fish-traps and so on. Along the front of the house there are platforms on which the padi is husked. Boats are stored under the house, and there the domestic animals, except the dogs, who inhabit the house, live. The house is reached by a sloping ladder cut out of a single log in such a way as to leave a hand-rail. The different tribes vary in the number of houses to a village; among some the village is made up of but one house.

Although these houses are so strongly built they

are not usually inhabited for long. The reason for moving them is either burning or a run of bad luck, or an epidemic or the exhaustion of the cultivated clearings, in which case the timbers are usually moved to the new site which has been chosen.

The clothing that the people wear is simple, and does not differ to any great extent among the different tribes. The most important garment worn by the men is the waist-cloth, over which out of doors they wear a coat of bark-cloth, or more frequently of trade cotton, and a sun-hat of palm leaves. Some also wear a small oblong mat of plaited rattan. At home they wear the waist-cloth and a band of rattan round the head. No man travels any distance from the house without his weapons—an oblong shield which is made of wood, a spear and a sword. Fire-arms, which have been recently introduced, form with the blow-pipe the only missile weapons they possess, unless we include the bow, which has a sporadic distribution as a toy in the north.

The dress of the women presents rather more variations. The general dress consists of a long sleeved jacket like that of the men, and a skirt of bark-cloth or cotton left open at the left side and reaching almost to the ankle. The Sea Dayak wear a corset of rattan, a jacket, and a short skirt which only reaches to the knee.

Transportation by water plays an important part in their economic life. They spend much time on the rivers, not only in going to and from the jungles in their hunting and other expeditions, but also going to their padi fields. Where the water is shallow, in the headwaters of a stream, they pole their boats; elsewhere the paddle is used. They make long journeys, and either visit friendly villages or camp on shore in a rude hut. Sometimes they tie up and roof the boat with mats.

The boats, no matter how big, are made out of a single log. These large boats are owned by the community, and have their freeboard raised by the lashing of additional planks. The freeboard in the middle of these larger boats is raised still higher and roofed in with palm leaves. About every three feet there are seats lashed with rattan to projections from the hull of the boat. The smaller boats owned by families only hold about seven or eight people and do not have the raised centre.

These peoples, except the wilder jungle tribes, engage in regular trade, especially with the Chinese. They sell the edible bird's nest, and are sufficiently acquainted with the habits of the traders to use currency. Their trade is like that of so many of the peoples I have discussed, the exchange of jungle products for luxuries, but unlike the others they have a more or less constant supply of rice and therefore are less dependent on barter to supplement their arts of life.

CHAPTER XV

LABOUR AND THE MAN

IN the studies which we have been pursuing we have seen how often the life of man is affected by his environment and how the arts of life react to geographical conditions. It has also appeared that certain conditions are particularly favourable for development. Labour reacts to the needs of man, to the available supplies, and also to the facilities for making the best use of those supplies. It shows a direct line of evolution, but it also progresses *per saltum* under the influence of contact with more advanced cultures.

It is natural that we should ask ourselves how far the converse is true, and whether labour, as represented by the arts of life, has reacted on man's physique. The question may be put in another way by inquiring how far mankind has specialized physically in order to carry on the arts of life more efficiently. It is of interest to raise the question whether the evolution of labour has been accompanied by a parallel evolution of man's form, and whether there can be said to be definite physical types which correspond to certain stages in the evolution of culture.

There can be little doubt that such specialization has occurred among the lower animals. While the whole organism has no doubt often changed, there seem to have been three factors which have had an extremely potent effect on the processes of evolution, the food quest, self-defence, and selection in relation to sex. The first two are of the greatest importance for our present purpose.

Many animals have survived owing to a specialization of the organs which are used for getting food. It is clear that the tongue of the ant-eater helps him to obtain his food, which might otherwise be difficult to reach. The speed with which the horses are endowed is of material advantage to them in escaping from their enemies. The physical perfection of the cats has been the subject of admiration among many naturalists, and has enabled the larger varieties to attain a supremacy which is unchallenged except by man.

At first sight it would appear as though mankind was singularly ill-fitted physically to stand the demands which his daily labour puts upon him, and that he has reacted but little to his daily tasks. In his primitive condition he seems to be naked, without great speed of foot or strength of claw. He cannot kill the game animals, on which he lives in the hunting stage, with his hands or his teeth. On the other hand man, and man alone, has succeeded in dominating nature, and there can be no doubt that the correlation between the organism and environment which has produced the evolution of the other animals has also affected the evolution of man. The matter is an extremely complicated one; it consists of a series of actions and reactions, the final result of which has been that man has become biologically speaking the most successful of all the animals and has been able even to control his environment, a feat performed by none of the other animals. We can study the whole question from the point of view of mankind as a whole, or from that of the individual. The more general question may be conveniently considered first.

Since the idea was first suggested, the theory that man is closely akin to the apes has been continuously confirmed by research. The line of development has been such that Klaatsch has stated that the ancestors of the modern apes were more anthropoid than their descendants, just as the ancestors of man were more ape-like than man is himself to-day.

In some ways it would appear, as is natural, that the apes are more specialized than man. The latter has, for instance, retained the hand of some very primitive ancestor.

The most primitive men, however, whom we know in any detail had specialized in a way which divides them very clearly from the apes. The least developed human fossil which has been discovered was found in Java. His remains show specialization in that feature which is most characteristic of man, namely, the brain. Considerable controversy has raged over the second point in which man differs most remarkably from the apes, namely, the upright gait. It seems probable that he walked in a semi-upright position. The same seems to have been true of Neanderthal man. The latter is of special interest to our purpose because we can associate him definitely with certain types of labour, namely, the earlier palæolithic industries. We may theorize, but we can say nothing definite about the correlation of the physique, especially the upright position and the brain, of the unknown ancestors of man with their surroundings, but in the case of Neanderthal man we can deal in facts.

We saw that the earlier industries differed from the later ones in palæolithic times. On the whole,

however, the evolution is fairly continuous, and the
break where it occurs hardly coincides with the great
change in physique which occurred in palæolithic
times. Neanderthal man constitutes a distinct race of
man, and the difference is so great that some observers
would be inclined to consider it as specific. Neanderthal man became extinct. He was therefore
biologically unsuccessful. The exact causes of his
extinction are uncertain and must probably remain
so for ever.

The race which succeeded him evolved we do not
know where or how at present. Our purpose here is
rather to inquire whether the conditions of labour which
followed are in any way to be correlated with the new
type. The differences which are most striking are in
the form of the face and of the jaws. The brain can
hardly be discussed, as the whole question of the
brain of fossil man is extremely controversial and
difficult, owing to the fact that endocranial casts can
only give us the form of the membranes which
enveloped the brain and not of the brain itself.

The face of Neanderthal man is remarkable for its
rugged strength. This is associated with a massive
jaw and a retreating forehead. Professor Thomson
has suggested that as the face forms the anvil on which
the jaw pounds it is necessary that when the pounding
is excessive the bony supports of the face should be
strong. This is especially necessary when the forehead is retreating and therefore does not provide an
elongated base to the anvil on which the jaw works,
as in the case of modern Europeans. The excessive
wear on the teeth and the weight of the jaw suggest
that Neanderthal man was specialized to use his jaws
in a way that is both unnecessary and impossible to
modern man. We may justifiably find in this jaw

and face development a correlation with the conditions of labour in early palæolithic times.

The teeth also show a specialization which points in the same direction. Sir Arthur Keith has pointed out that they have an enlarged pulp cavity which extends deep into the jaw. The teeth are thus very firmly wedged into their sockets, and are able to withstand the strain which the eating of coarse food put upon them. It is worth noting here that man's teeth are, except for the development of the enlarged cavity, of a comparatively unspecialized character. The great development of the canines, which is so characteristic of the larger apes and which no doubt assisted them both in fighting and in tearing their food, is entirely absent. Man under primitive conditions moved his jaws sideways as well as up and down. The special form of the teeth of Neanderthal man seems to be an adaptation to this special form of mastication. His bones are all very massive, a possible necessity under conditions where life was undoubtedly very hard.

In suggesting that there is in Neanderthal man a correlation between occupations and the physical form of the body it must be remembered that modern theories in no way support the suggestion which has become associated with the name of Lamarck, that a certain physical feature can be developed in an individual through use and subsequently inherited. It seems more probable that animals, including of course man, have certain potentialities, some of which may appear in response to environmental or other conditions.

Such a theory would explain the presence in man, ancient or modern, of what may be called simian characters. It may be suggested that in many cases they are not "throw backs" but the response of the organism to a particular environment which was normal in remote times but which may repeat itself under modern conditions. In this way we can explain the resemblance in certain ways of the Australians to Neanderthal man by a similarity, limited it is true, but none the less of importance to the work that Mousterian man and the Australian aborigines both had to perform.

We have insufficient data at present to correlate the advance of palæolithic culture in the second half of that age with the changed form of physique. The presence of skulls with negroid characters at Grimaldi has led Sollas to make a very interesting parallel of the Aurignacians and the Bushmen. He admits, however, that the parallel must not be pressed too closely, as it seems very improbable that the Grimaldi race had a wide distribution in Europe.

The Langwith Bassett cranium may be cited in this connexion. This cranium, which is now in the department of Human Anatomy in Oxford, was discovered in a cave in Derbyshire by the Rev. G. H. Mullins. There can be little doubt that the cave was at one time inhabited by Aurignacian man as the remains of his hearths. The cranium was found in a corner of the cave by an overhanging ledge. I examined the site of the find under the guidance of the discoverer, and came to the conclusion that the archæological evidence was unsatisfactory. The bones were probably carried to that position by water, which had no doubt been the agency by which the greater part of the cave had been filled with earth and bones.

The cranium has certain primitive features and may possibly belong to the Aurignacian age, and therefore be contemporary with the hearths. On the other hand we have no good evidence to suggest that it does. The condition of the bone leaves no doubt that it is extremely ancient, but beyond this it is impossible to go. When we have more ancient crania from this country it may be possible on morphological grounds to assign a definite date. At present, however, owing to the uncertainty of the archæological evidence, we must unfortunately refrain from assigning a definite period to this most important human document.

In the Magdalenian period we are more fortunate, and if we examine the osseous remains of man which are definitely associated with that phase of human progress we have evidence which is very suggestive, if not of the reaction or correlation of labour or a race, at least of the effect on physique of certain conditions which make for a definite culture. Our evidence is unfortunately based on insufficient skeletal material for us to put forward a hypothesis which can be other than tentative.

Two types of men seem to be associated with the Magdalenian period; they are called from the place where they were found, Cromagnon and Chancelade man. The former presents characters which were considered by Pruner Bey to be Mongoloid. It has not been suggested at present that we can correlate this type of man with any conditions either of environment or of culture. With Chancelade man the case is otherwise. The characters of this skeleton, for we are unfortunately limited to a single skeleton, are such that it seems highly probable that morphologically at least we are in the presence of bones which are almost the exact counterpart of those possessed by the modern Eskimo. Summing up the principal characters, it may be noted that both the Eskimo and Chancelade man have long narrow heads with a peculiar ridge at the top of the cranial vault. Both have long narrow noses, wide orbits and long narrow palates. The form of the face is also similar.

In order to explain these similarities we may adopt two attitudes : either the Eskimo are of the same race as Magdalenian man or else similar conditions either of labour or of environment make for a similar type. It is also possible to adopt a combination of these two hypotheses and to suggest, on the basis of the evidence of Cromagnon man, that at this time we had in Europe a Mongoloid strain, and that the convergence of the Eskimo and of the Chancelade man is due to the fact that they both belong to the same race, and therefore it is natural that given certain environmental conditions they should resemble one another.

There seems good reason to suppose, as Thomson[1] has suggested, that the peculiar form of the Eskimo skull with its pent-house top is due to the great development of the temporal muscles, which by continual use drag it into this shape. The Eskimo from their youth up put a very great strain on their jaws by continually chewing skins. Owing to the rigorous climate this is the only available means of rendering them supple and fit for use. It seems not impossible that under similar Arctic conditions the Magdalenians may have pursued a similar method. The development of the teeth and palate may possibly also be associated with this habit, and possibly also with the hardness of their diet. It is natural to suppose that a diet of frozen meat or fish would be apt to tax the jaws to a very considerable extent.

The form of the nose appears to be closely correlated

---

[1] I am very much indebted in what follows to the teaching of Professor Arthur Thomson, in whose department it has been my good fortune to work since undergraduate days, and who has on very many occasions discussed with me the problems raised in this chapter.

with climatic conditions.[1] Where the air is cold the nose tends to be narrow and converse. Excessive humidity also tends to be correlated with a broad nose and dryness with a narrow nose, but humidity is a less potent factor than temperature. The narrowness of the Eskimo nose seems to be in close harmony with Arctic conditions, and it may reasonably be suggested that similar factors were at work in the case of Chancelade man. If this be so, we have here a very good example of certain environmental factors being responsible both for a peculiar culture and also for a feature in man's physique.

The form of the face is closely related both to the organs of respiration and of mastication, and here also we might expect, if what has been said above proves to be correct, that the face of both Chancelade man and of the Eskimo resemble one another owing to the influence both of similar climatic conditions and of similar culture, the latter being no doubt developed under these very rigorous climatic conditions.

If we leave prehistoric times and consider the effect of various cultures on modern man we are face to face here also with certain very interesting problems. In general terms it must be clearly understood that man's physique is more conservative than his culture. Culture-contact often has an immediate and direct result and completely transforms the arts of a race. The mixing of races proceeds much more slowly. It is possible in a comparatively short time completely to change the material arts of any people. On the other hand we do not know how long it takes for one race completely to absorb another.

---

[1] Thomson and Buxton, " Man's Nasal Index in Relation to Certain Climatic Conditions," Jour. Roy. Anthr. Inst., LIII (1923), p. 92.

There is a Chinese proverb which states that China is a sea which salts all that comes into it. There can be little doubt that the dominant culture of the Chinese Empire has absorbed many strange racial elements, and that most of them are now indistinguishable from the mass of the Chinese. We do not know, however, how far these strangers have changed the original Chinese type, nor again how far a similar culture, similar environment, and similar types of labour may have made for a similar physique. Certain types of culture have been associated with the Mediterranean race, that is the long-headed short brunets, who inhabit Southern Europe and parts of Asia. Here again we are in doubt as to whether the culture-complex is correlated with the race and forms its inheritance or whether the physical type may not be correlated with a certain culture-complex, by no means the same thing. It is not even perfectly certain that there is any correlation at all.

It has been shown that there is a very definite correlation between certain classes of labour and the sexes. Heavier labour is man's work and lighter labour woman's work. It also appears to be true that certain aptitudes do seem to be associated with the sexes. We can, however, hardly affirm that this is the result of evolution or selective adaptation to particular types of labour, because we find that among different races the same type of labour may be associated with sex.

It is by no means impossible that man's work and woman's work may have reacted on each other, and that to a certain extent they may have pursued a separate line of development. Mankind appears to behave biologically as plants and animals do under domestication, and we know that female characters are transmissible through the male, and that it is possible to breed the sexes in certain directions. It is therefore possible that a similar, though unconscious, process may have been taking place in mankind, and what I have called in an earlier chapter the fundamental division of labour may not have reacted on physique. At present, however, the matter must await further research.

In dealing with the problem of the reaction of labour on various races we are still on uncertain ground. There can be little doubt that just in the same way that various groups of animals have become extinct, owing probably to their failure to adjust themselves to new conditions, so various tribes have disappeared. In the case of animals the problem seems to be a purely biological one. Failure to react physically to environment means extinction, but the race which can adapt itself to the changed conditions survives. With man it is possible that matters may be otherwise.

There are two possibilities. In the first place survival may be due to an adaptation to the purely physical environment. In this case we should expect to find among men that certain types were dominant under certain types of climate, and others where the climate or the environmental conditions imposed by nature were different. To a certain extent this condition holds good. We find, for instance, that, generally speaking, skin colour does appear to be correlated with certain types of climate. The same holds good for the nasal index, and it would be possible to multiply further examples. There are, however, numerous exceptions to these correlations. The adaptation of physique to environment does not appear to be the only factor which makes for survival.

Considerable stress has been laid on disease and its effect on the survival of certain races. The great aim of the breeders of certain plants is to produce a strain which shall be resistant to disease. Recently Shipley[1] has pointed out how after a very long period a certain type of sugar-cane suddenly succumbed to a particular disease. There is evidence which abundantly proves the wholesale destruction of primitive races by introduced forms of disease. In many cases it would appear as if certain diseases were to be associated with certain types of culture, and it would almost appear as if immunity to them were the by-product of certain types of culture-complexes. I am speaking, of course, of specific and not of occupational diseases. When a migrant people introduces together with its culture into the virgin field of another race a disease of this type, it not infrequently happens that the race which had not established immunity to the disease dies out, or is at least decimated before it can adopt the new culture.

There is a further factor which has an important bearing on the extinction of races. It would seem as though each culture were correlated with a definite type of group feeling, the natural outcome of that self-consciousness which is the most remarkable quality of man. This group feeling is definitely associated with a certain culture-complex, and includes both the spiritual and the material sides of the culture. When, as has been pointed out by Rivers, the indigenous culture is threatened by a dominant alien culture, it may happen that the tribe loses the will to live and so becomes extinct. It is of importance, therefore, to emphasize the fact that a type of culture can have a very definite correlation with the physique

[1] *The Times*, April 21st, 1924.

of a people indirectly by affecting their group psychology.

If we consider the extremely slow rate at which population has increased we must postulate various wholesale destructions of great magnitude in relation to the population. The experience of the comparatively destructive effect of the Great War, incomparably man's greatest destructive effort, with that of the influenza epidemic makes it clear that disease may have played a very important part. The effect of the psychological destruction of a race has not yet been measured. It will probably prove to be great.

It will be seen, then, that it is probable that the evolution of culture has an intimate association with the survival or the extinction of a race, much in the same way that certain physical characters can be shown to ensure the survival of a certain type of organism. The greatest period of advance usually follows a period in which destruction has taken place. Those individuals or groups which survive the catastrophe seem better fitted to make advances than the whole mass before the catastrophe took place. Culture-contact and racial admixture is normally attended either by the disappearance of the less capable race or else by a burst of great progress. It would seem therefore as if side by side with the beneficent effect of racial admixture the mixing of cultures probably reacted on the racial physique.

In addition to possible effects in relation to the physical survival or destruction of certain tribes, it is probable that a definite type of labour among primitive peoples may under certain conditions make for the diffusion of a particular racial type, with the result that this type either becomes altered to suit a new environment or else imposes at least part of its physical characters upon another people. In dealing with geographical conditions I have referred to the extraordinary sensitiveness of oasis dwellers to particular conditions in the oasis. The life there makes for a big population and one of great density. When conditions change the very culture which caused a big population compels them to seek homes elsewhere. In this way we have at various times in Asia had great migrations of folk from the oases into the fringing grass-lands. In this way the culture and the physique of very big areas have been changed.

But it is not only in oases where these phenomena have been taking place. Wherever natural conditions and the advance of culture have made a big increase in population possible, sooner or later, unless some castastrophe occurred, it has been necessary for the population to find an outlet into some less densely populated area. The effect of such migrations on the populations of the world has been of the very greatest. Even under favourable natural conditions, however, such an increase in the population is hardly possible except with the assistance of a type of culture which can take advantage of such conditions. The spread therefore of certain types of man over the world may be said to be very largely the result of the evolution of more productive types of labour.

It will be found that the most primitive types of culture are usually to be found among more isolated folk who are less advanced physically. An advanced culture has on the other hand enabled certain races to impose their physique over a very wide area. It is true that we are often at a loss to distinguish cause and effect, but it is true that higher cultures appear to be correlated with a more advanced type of physique. It is also clear that in some cases at least the higher culture, in spite of a physique which is not apparently suited to the environment, has succeeded more or less in establishing itself because of the advantages conferred by the physique. To a certain extent, therefore, in this direction at least labour does make the man.

If we abandon the field of generalities and endeavour to associate a definite type with various grades of labour we shall be less successful. If labour left its direct mark on races we ought to be able to distinguish a certain physical type among hunters, herdsmen and agriculturalists. To do this is hardly possible, and he would be a very bold man who, from an examination of the data provided by a series of skeletons, were to pronounce on the exact state of culture which their possessors had reached. Within limits, however, even here it may be said that labour has reacted on the physical form.

The more primitive races, that is to say those who are living in the collecting stage, are usually to be distinguished both for the massive size of their teeth, which seems to be an inherited character, and may be described, if we so will, as " racial," and also in the wear to which those teeth have been subjected, an individual character. These differences, marked as they are, appear to be the result of a combination of actions and reactions, but there can be little doubt that the eating of coarse food is correlated with strength of teeth and jaw. Here again it should be pointed out that in all probability a massive jaw is one of the potentialities of the human race as a whole, and that under certain conditions of environment, using this word in the widest sense, it becomes a dominant character.

The special character of the face among the

Mongoloid races is remarkable, and may possibly be correlated with certain mechanical stresses that are put upon the masticatory apparatus. Among them the muscles which are used to move the jaw up and down are comparatively feebly developed, whereas those which move the jaw from side to side have a great development. The development of these latter muscles is usually associated with a shallow glenoid fossa, the socket into which the jaw fits. This shallowness is not limited to those races where the up and down movement is feeble, for it also occurs, as Knowles[1] has shown, among the Eskimo. It seems, however, to be always associated with a definite shearing movement of the jaws, which may or may not be accompanied by movement in a vertical direction. It is remarkable, however, that the shallowness of the glenoid fossa seems nearly always to be associated with a buttressing of the face.

The distribution of this form of face is wide, including as it does most of the inhabitants of Asia and the aborigines of North America. The shallow glenoid is closely connected with a hard manner of life. I had occasion recently to examine a number of skulls, probably of pre-Aztec date, from the Valley of Mexico. Among them both the shallowness of the glenoid and the buttressing of the flat face was very remarkable. Unlike the Eskimo, these people seem to have made little use of the vertical movements of the jaws. Tentatively, it may be suggested that, to a certain extent at least, the eating of maize, possibly insufficiently cooked, is not uncorrelated with their remarkable jaw development. It is not impossible that the eating of cereals in large quantities, a form of diet

[1] Knowles, " Mem. of the Canadian Geological Survey," No. 9.

which necessitates a great deal of mastication, may be associated with the form of face and jaw so characteristic of Eastern Asia.

If we compare civilized and primitive man we see most clearly how culture does seem to react on the form of the face. Limited as we are to the study of primitive man it is unnecessary to consider these differences in detail. The directions in which they proceed are in the reduction of the size of the face and of the jaws and palate. It seems not unreasonable to suggest that improved standards of living and softer food are correlated with these reductions.

The limbs also show certain differences which are to be associated directly with the reaction of culture on mankind. I have already referred to the different gait which is characteristic of some primitive peoples. Associated with primitive peoples we find a flattening of the bones of the thigh and the leg. It is not impossible that this flattening is due to their peculiar gait. The contrast between them and civilized man is also increased by the habit of going barefoot, or at the most of wearing a soft shoe of the moccasin type. Thomson has shown that those peoples who habitually squat on their haunches instead of sitting on chairs develop supernumerary facets on the bones of the lower limb. These are, of course, not to be considered as racial characters, but more probably as characters which are acquired by each individual during the course of his life. They may be considered as a very definite reaction of labour on the human frame. These differences, however, do not seem to be associated with any particular race or environment, but rather with primitive peoples generally.

The distribution of similar arts of life among widely divergent races serves to show in spite of what has been said above that, taken in the mass, labour seems to show but little correlation with race, with the important qualifications which have been detailed above. On the other hand we do find that the white race has certain features which would seem to suggest that the passage from a primitive to a more advanced stage has not been without reaction on the human frame. There can be little doubt that the direct influence of climate is intimately correlated with race.

The food supply is probably another important factor, and it has been seen how closely all forms of culture are also bound up with the food supply. It seems more than probable that the indirect action of labour necessary to make use of the food supply has also helped to mould the characters of the various races. At present, however, our knowledge of physical anthropology is insufficient accurately to answer this question.

If we turn to the individual we find that it is possible far more accurately to gauge the effect of labour on man. The callous upon the hands of those who are accustomed to hard manual labour is a familiar case in point. But the effects of labour are deeper. The skeleton itself usually bears very definite marks of the type of labour in which the individual was engaged. The physiological effects of hard labour under different conditions are usually marked, especially among most primitive races.

Man as a race, and as an individual, has been able to adapt himself to and to triumph over his environment in a way that no other animal has succeeded in doing. He has developed a self-consciousness which marks him off from the rest of nature. It is easy with the evidence before us to estimate the effect which his labour has had on nature. He has even in primitive times been able to change his environment to an astonishing degree. It seems highly probable that the artificial environment which is the result of the labour of his hands has in turn reacted on him, and still continues so to react. For the present, however, although we are conscious of this reaction, and to a certain extent can even measure it, the time does not seem to have arrived when we can generalize on it with any great degree of certainty.

The continued action of the forces which we have been discussing will probably have certain well marked effects in the future. It seems not impossible that a large number of the more primitive races are doomed to extinction, even though civilized man is making great efforts to preserve them. The diffusion of cultures and the concomitant mixing of races is likely also profoundly to affect the racial stocks in certain parts of the world. It remains to be seen how far modern science will enable the white man to oust the coloured races from certain parts of the world where up to the present the coloured are alone biologically successful. The work which has been done at Panama shows how the organized labour of a cultured community can enable members of that community to survive where formerly they died; and proves conclusively the important biological effect of organized labour on mankind.

We have but few data at present which enable us to surmise how far the human frame will react to advancing conditions of culture. Duckworth [1] suggests that possibly microscopic changes will take place in the structure of the brain. At the same time he points out

[1] The whole question is discussed by him in the last chapter of his "Morphology and Anthropology."

that in the other organs it is impossible that the reduction, for instance in the jaw, should continue beyond a certain minimum stage necessary for the proper functioning of the body.

As a general conclusion we may say that the evolution of labour has been a comparatively speedy process, and the time which man has taken to raise himself from the crudest culture to an advanced stage has been, geologically speaking, rapid. Man's physique seems to have been more conservative in its development, but at the same time, while it is undoubtedly true that man has made labour, it seems not improbable that in its reaction labour has played no mean part in fashioning man.

INDEX